Robert De Niro

Robert De Niro

Anatomy of an Actor

CAHIERS DU
CINEMA

Robert De Niro

Glenn Kenny

Introduction

"What I gotta do?"
—Jake La Motta in *Raging Bull*

Even the best, most astute critics have a largely unfortunate tendency to manufacture mythologies for their subjects. Of course, when a subject pulls off mythical feats, that tendency can be particularly difficult to squelch. Hence the primary challenge of dealing with Robert De Niro. It is difficult to deny him the status of a performing Prometheus. Certain of his achievements are practically unprecedented in the history of acting, either on stage or on the screen.

In the late 1970s, De Niro worked with Martin Scorsese—the director with whom his best work is often associated and with whom he shares strong bonds in terms of background and affinities—on *Raging Bull*, a movie based on the life of the middleweight boxer Jake La Motta, an Italian-American son of the Bronx who was most active in the forties and fifties, and who was best known for his ferocity in the ring and, later, his self-defeating and brutal behavior in life. *Raging Bull* would depict the boxer both in his best and most fearsome fighting shape and then, as La Motta let himself fall apart, as an overweight lout who eventually finds a form of peace. The problem De Niro and Scorsese set themselves to solving was how to portray La Motta in the latter phase of his life. In the past, the physical transformations of characters on stage or screen were accomplished by means of makeup or some form of prosthetics. The director and his star consulted with filmmaker Michael Powell, who was a mentor to Scorsese. Three decades earlier, Powell had directed the romantic epic *The Life and Death of Colonel Blimp* (1943), in which Roger Livesey played the lead role as a dashing, lean young officer at the turn of the nineteenth century and a rather walrus-like military fogey during the Second World War. "Marty asked me how I managed Roger Livesey's weight gain in *Colonel Blimp*," Powell wrote in the second part of his autobiography. "How did we turn a young, fit, springy guardsman into an old, pink, sweating walrus? I told him it was partly makeup, and partly by using doubles."[1] These methods were not satisfactory to De Niro. "*Raging Bull* took a long time because Bobby wanted to put on all the weight," Scorsese recounted. "We had to shut down and pay the entire crew for about four months while he ate his way around Northern Italy and France. He said it was hard to get up in the morning and force yourself to have breakfast, then lunch, then dinner. After a while it became really uncomfortable for him."[2]

The Two Jakes

The result was, and remains, staggering. The contrast between the two La Mottas is made plain very early in the film, which opens with the title card "New York City 1964" and then shows the overweight La Motta in evening dress, preparing for his nightclub act. The actor, De Niro, is wearing makeup, to be sure: he has a puffed-up nose and a receding hairline that makes his brow look like a block of concrete. But his bulk and the actual shape of his head: these things are real. He lights a cigar, goes over some of his lines. The shot cuts from a medium view, taking in a lot of the dressing room, to a medium close-up. La Motta/De Niro is not what you would nowadays call "morbidly obese," but he's very much overweight; his heavy breathing isn't just on account of his puffs on his cigar. As if to remind the viewer, a title appears below his face: "Jake La Motta 1964." The movie then cuts, quickly, to the inside of a boxing ring, and the contrast is startling: a sweaty man with a nearly full head of hair and a less bulbous nose, in a boxing crouch. The face is lean. Its jawline, pretty much all flabby chin in the prior view, is now long and sharp; the eyes, so sleepy before, are alert, intent. The title card on this medium close-up is "Jake La Motta 1941." The viewer barely has time to take this in before the face in the frame takes two powerhouse punches.

But the illusion is convincing and complete. And of course neither of these men is Jake La Motta, and the years are not 1964 and 1941. The scenes featuring the boxing La Motta were begun in spring of 1979; photography on the "fat" scenes was completed around Christmas of that year. Both views are of Robert De Niro in 1979.

"I was shocked," Michael Powell said about learning of De Niro's weight-gain scheme. "It wasn't necessary. It wasn't right, it was a very risky thing to do."[3]

Robert De Niro
in New York in 1973.

Furthermore, the precedent set in *Raging Bull* introduced into the Hollywood acting mainstream a very specific notion of the body as malleable instrument, and De Niro's descendants have made a veritable industry, via trainers and specialized physicians and nutritionists, of physical modification for "the work." (Christian Bale lost sixty pounds for the psychological horror picture *The Machinist* [2004], to cite but one example.)

If what De Niro did for *Raging Bull* set a precedent, it was not a precedent for De Niro himself. "Bobby is the most complete actor I know," Shelley Winters, another product of the New York stage and proponent of certain techniques that have fallen (with accuracy or not) under the umbrella of "Method acting," observed in 1975. "When we did *Bloody Mama* he played my youngest son who was a junkie. By the time we got done filming, he had lost 30 pounds and broken out in sores all over his body. After he got killed in the script, I was afraid I'd look in the grave during the burial scene and find him."[4] It's worth remembering that *Bloody Mama* was a 1970 low-budget gangster film directed by the ultrapragmatic Roger Corman, who certainly did not ask De Niro to do as he did. There's something in the way Winters tells the story that makes one imagine that he did it in just as solitary and as focused a way as his *Taxi Driver* character Travis Bickle carved Xes into the tops of his bullets before embarking on his killing spree.

Or is that really true? The above simile arguably buys into a certain mythology of De Niro, a mythology that is now on the wane, or, perhaps one ought to say, in flux. In 2000, in an introduction to a 1996 De Niro profile for British *Esquire* anthologized in his *The Nick Tosches Reader*, Tosches, himself no slouch at self-mythologizing, observed, "On the few occasions when Robert De Niro had spoken to the press through the years, his words and manner of speaking had always been mangled and edited to a false neatness and comprehensibility. In this piece [...] I wanted to capture his true voice and his singular manner of trying to openly express what remains articulated inside him."[5] Mm-hmm. De Niro's reluctance to do interviews, and his seeming stumbling while doing them, his famous taciturnity in contrast to his preternaturally vivid presence on screen, created a mythology that itself spawned a counter-mythology. It made De Niro as famous for being an enigma, a code that a journalist or critic with just the right amount of persistence and perspicacity could crack. But what if the answer is in front of our faces, and always has been? "Robert De Niro is one of a select number of actors I've directed who work hard at their trade, and the only one who asked to rehearse on Sundays," Elia Kazan recalled. "Most of the others play tennis."[6]

Kazan directed De Niro in *The Last Tycoon* (1976), a handsomely mounted but ultimately emotionally unrealized adaptation of F. Scott Fitzgerald's unfinished novel about a brilliant Hollywood moviemaker Fitzgerald had based on Irving Thalberg. De Niro had never played a character as cerebral as Monroe Stahr. Kazan recognized this. "My problem with De Niro was to transform a New York Italian kid into 'Hollywood royalty,' a thin, somewhat sickly Jew with erudition and culture," Kazan writes in his autobiography. "That wasn't easy. I didn't know much about Bobby—our coming together had been on instinct, his and mine— but we immediately understood each other. Bobby, a tough kid, was capable, like Marlon, of extraordinary sensitivity in a performance. Like me, he would do almost anything to succeed [...]."[7]

In the early part of De Niro's career as a leading man, when his gift seemed to burn brightest, the effectiveness of his work was also, paradoxically enough, seemingly dependent on the strength of the movie he was in. He did not give the kind of performance that could "save" a movie. He could only dazzle in a movie that dazzled. Kazan and company did not pull that off for *The Last Tycoon*. Kazan mentions "Marlon," and of course Brando is one of the actors to whom De Niro is most frequently compared. And yet in their particulars they are exceptionally different performers. For much of his early performing career Brando traded on his substantial sexual allure, which is entirely understandable; De Niro, whose good looks are not old Hollywood but nonetheless solid, did not. The opening salvo of Brando's screen career was playing the surly, sultry stud Stanley Kowalski in Kazan's film of *A Streetcar Named Desire* (1951). In his most notable early roles De Niro played characters who were either perversely dysfunctional (his recurring character Jon Rubin in Brian De Palma's late-sixties and early-seventies films *Greetings* [1968] and *Hi, Mom!* [1970] is a voyeur) or simply had no relation to sexuality (his Johnny Boy in Scorsese's *Mean Streets* barely exists in relation to other people at all, never mind women). Whatever feminine side De Niro may have in life, it almost never manifests itself in performance as it does in much of Brando's work (note the particulars of the latter's vulnerability in, say, *On the Waterfront* [1954]), nor does De Niro's on-screen aura ever leave behind even a whiff of evanescent poetry in the Brando manner.

Of the ten films that this study examines in specific detail, I argue that six of them are motion pictures in which the actor and the work are inextricably linked, where one is almost unimaginable without the other. Those of course would include all four of the collaborations with director Martin Scorsese in the ten: *Mean Streets*, *Taxi Driver*, *Raging Bull*, and *The King of Comedy*. I also put Francis Ford Coppola's

Robert De Niro in *Bloody Mama* (1970), the low-budget gangster movie directed by Roger Corman.

Top: With William Finley and
Charles Pfluger in *The
Wedding Party* (1969),
directed by Brian De Palma
and Wilford Leach.

Bottom: Playing Jon Rubin
in another De Palma film,
Greetings, released the
previous year.

The Godfather Part II in that category, and the
final film of the ten, 2010's *Stone*, a picture that
in many respects gives the lie to the notion that
his performance powers are direly diminished.
The other four are pictures in which, for better or
worse, he functions as a notable feature, or even
an emblem. While these are, not unexpectedly,
largely grouped among the latter pictures of
his career, I would also include the 1973 *Bang
the Drum Slowly*, the picture that made critics
and the industry sit up and take notice, in this
category, as I do *Midnight Run*, his 1988 bid for
movie stardom rather than cinephile/thespian
cult figure, and of course *Awakenings* and *Meet
the Parents*. One can't really begin to understand
what De Niro is about as a performer without
examining these, despite the fact that for many
who revere the De Niro who played Jake
La Motta, the De Niro mugging at comic actor
Ben Stiller is painful to witness.

"Droll De Niro"

The dismantling of the De Niro myth began
almost two decades ago, more than thirty years
after he first stood in front of a movie camera.
"Droll De Niro," the astute, unforgiving critic
Gilbert Adair snarked in his 1995 book *Flickers*.
"For what a curious figure Robert De Niro is.
The finest actor of the American cinema's post-
Brando generation (Nicholson, Hoffman, Pacino,
etc.), he has also, perversely, seemed determined
to emulate Brando's pitiful decline into numbing
repetition and outright eccentricity. So statufied,
in recent years, have his patented tics become, one
has sometimes had the impression of watching
him give, as though on stage rather than screen,
his thousandth weary performance of the same
part. Indeed, one cannot help but wonder whether,
even in terms of strictly physical transformation,
the role he played in Martin Scorsese's *Raging
Bull* (already all of fifteen years ago!) might
have been a premonitory allegory for his own
subsequent deterioration as a performer."[8]

The Disappointments

Obviously, De Niro did change—people are
known to do that—and he laid his career down
tracks that tended to serve what could be
described as his own interests rather than those
of the muse of acting or whomever. Playing
tough guy for comic effect in 1988's *Midnight
Run*, which also happened to be the biggest
commercial success of his career until that point,
was an indicator. Subsequent films did not
necessarily suggest that he was always going to
shy away from the 100-proof, but an increasing
tilt toward the comedic intimated to some
observers a flirtation with self-parody; the worst
fears of those fans and critics were confirmed
when De Niro went so far as to reprise Travis

Bickle's immortal taunt "You talkin' to me?" in
the guise of "Fearless Leader" in a wretched live-
action adaptation of the *Rocky and Bullwinkle*
cartoon. *Meet the Parents* is one thing—playing
a threatening old-school father-in-law to Ben
Stiller's well-intentioned but hopelessly nebbishy
fiancé of De Niro's daughter was a not entirely
disreputable way of exercising his comic chops,
as we'll see in the chapter devoted to that picture.
But the subsequent mini-franchise, in which the
likes of Dustin Hoffman and Barbra Streisand are
roped in to squander their dignity, is something
wholly other.

Those determined to wallow in De Niro
disappointment will also note that the actor is an
executive producer on many of the pictures that
let them down, making them more than mere
"paycheck" jobs for better or worse. Indeed, the
actor's entrepreneurial side, which emerged into
more public view after he cofounded the Tribeca
Film Festival in an attempt to bolster business
in his own New York neighborhood after the
9/11 attacks, seems, at least to some, to consume
more of De Niro's energy and ingenuity these
days than does acting. But he remains a working
actor, and one of the best we've got, and there's
something that we civilians ought to understand
about working actors: they like to work. De Niro
continues to work not at the behest of worshipers
at the temple of cinema. He works because he's
an actor. And he takes money gigs because he's
an actor who's also a businessman. The extent to
which this is laudable or worthy of condemnation
is not, finally, a matter for this study. The work
and its multiple aspects are.

The Facts

Elia Kazan called De Niro a "street kid;" that's
not inaccurate. But he was a street kid with
a difference: both of his parents were artists.
Robert De Niro Sr. was a largely abstract
expressionist painter and sculptor whose work
was exhibited alongside that of Pollack and
Rothko in the forties, and who continued to show
his work widely even as his son's fame eclipsed
his respectable reputation. De Niro Jr.'s mother,
Virginia Admiral, was also a poet and painter, but
after she divorced De Niro Sr. when their son was
an infant she mainly did clerical work to support
herself and her son.

De Niro Jr. was born on August 17, 1943, and
raised around the East Village, Little Italy, and the
area now known as SoHo. Discussing his formal
introduction to De Niro, Elizabeth Street–raised
Martin Scorsese recalled that he had known him
from the old neighborhood: "[H]e used to hang
out with a different group of people, on Broome
Street, while we were on Prince Street. We had
seen each other at dances and said hello."[9] De
Niro Jr., taciturn on all subjects at the outset of his
career, has been almost ferociously protective of

the facts of his childhood. In De Niro's first major interview, with Lawrence Grobel for *Playboy*, Grobel meticulously details every time De Niro turns off Grobel's tape recorder to speak off the record or to balk at a line of questioning. He does this most often when Grobel asks about his childhood, whether he ran with gangs, why he got the nickname "Bobby Milk" (depending on which subsequent account you read/believe, it's either because he drank a lot of milk or because he had pale skin), and so on.

The information that at the age of ten he played the Cowardly Lion in a production of *The Wizard of Oz* is, naturally, deemed pertinent. He was a shy kid, and acting was seen as a way to perhaps break out of that mode, and De Niro pursued the work seriously from his teens on, dropping out of high school not to loaf but to go and study at the Actors Studio and with Stella Adler at her conservatory. Initially De Niro merely audited Adler's classes. "My mother did some work—typing and proofreading manuscripts—for Maria Ley-Piscator, the wife of Erwin Piscator, who founded the Dramatic Workshop," De Niro told Grobel. "She knew I wanted to go to acting school, so in exchange for my mother's work, I began going on Saturdays. It was the biggest acting school in the city at that time. Stella Adler [...] had a very good script-breakdown-and-analysis class that no one else was teaching [...]."[10]

De Niro worked on the New York stage, and in touring companies, but had been movie-mad as a kid, and was not yet twenty years old when he auditioned for a part in a film being made by a small collective led by a professor at Sarah Lawrence College and two of his more promising students, one of whom was Brian De Palma. "Nobody knew him," De Palma recalled in 1975, speaking while on a visit to the set of Scorsese's *Taxi Driver*. "He was only a kid of 19. He read for the movie and then asked to do an improvisation from *Waiting for Lefty*. He went out and then came back in like a powerhouse. He came on like Broderick Crawford—reading a speech to the cabbies in the union hall. He was simply great—that I remember."[11]

The movie, shot in 1963, was a New Wave inflected comedy called *The Wedding Party*, in which De Niro, sporting close-cropped hair and shirtsleeves, played Cecil, a roughneck pal of the movie's groom who tries to talk the lead character down from the marriage ledge. De Niro is pretty deft in the role and appears far more at ease than in his next outing with De Palma in *Greetings* some five years later. The picture didn't see any kind of release until 1969. In the interim De Niro got work in one of the late films of the great French director Marcel Carné, the US-shot *Trois chambres à Manhattan* (1965), in a bit as a diner patron. Ironically, in the early seventies De Niro signed up to do a role that Al Pacino, an actor he is frequently linked with for a variety of reasons (the most

recurrent of which recently has been along the lines of "I can't believe this great actor is wasting his talent in [movie X],"), dropped out of in order to make *The Godfather*: that of Mario in *The Gang That Couldn't Shoot Straight* (1971), the misbegotten adaptation of Jimmy Breslin's comic novel of Mafia ineptitude. De Niro's experience on this film would, at least for a period, inform his perspective on his career choices.

In recent years his reasons, when he deigns to share them, have been informed by his life choices perhaps more than strictly artistic ones. For instance, he cites late-in-life fatherhood—he sired twins in 1995 and a son in 1998—as part of his motivation for participating in the above-mentioned *The Adventures of Rocky and Bullwinkle* (2000) and the animated *Shark Tale* (2004). For up until that point he had made few films that any children could or ought to be allowed to see, let alone his own. (The main problem with *Rocky and Bullwinkle*, and to an arguably lesser extent *Shark Tale*, is that they ended up being movies that *no one* should see.) In any event, it is in many respects fitting that the beginnings of the De Niro myth arise in a film in which the New York City street kid transforms himself in to a good-hearted son of the South.

Robert De Niro in the title role of *The Last Tycoon* (1976), directed by Elia Kazan.

1

Bruce Pearson

Bang the Drum Slowly (1973)
John Hancock

"I always been pretty much of a nobody."
—Bruce Pearson

The Wedding Party, in which De Niro excelled playing a quasi-roughneck pal of the story's prospective groom, introduced De Niro to director Brian De Palma, who would prove an important collaborator. The movie's protracted editing process held up its release, so it couldn't get any traction for the actor's film career. De Niro spent much of the 1960s doing a motley array of theatrical work.

The drag performer Holly Woodlawn, an Andy Warhol "superstar" of that decade, is likely one of dozens in the New York arts world with an "I gave Robert De Niro his first break" anecdote. In 2003 Woodlawn "waxed nostalgic" to columnist Liz Smith: "After noting that she had sent him a get-well card as he recovered from prostate cancer, she took credit for getting Bobby his first acting job. As Holly tells it, it was during the production of *Glamour, Glory and Gold*, a way Off-Broadway effort that also starred another Warhol goddess, Candy Darling. 'Bobby's mom owned a printing shop in Brooklyn,' Holly said. 'We didn't have the money to make up posters, so Ron Link, the director, and myself, told Mrs. De Niro, "We will make your son a star, on one condition: you print up the posters for free!"' The rest, according to Holly, is history. (De Niro played all 10 of the male roles in this little late '60s show.)"[12]

There were other shows and tours. In the file on De Niro at the New York Public Library, Performing Arts Division, the very first clipping on De Niro dates from May 3, 1967, and is from the *Guilford Gazette*, a North Carolina paper. Gene S. Key reviews a touring production of the play *Tchin-Tchin*, and notes "Of the lot though, the Niro [sic] must be singled out, as he revealed the anguish of a lost soul, uneducated and uncultured, trying to find the way in a complicated world that had heretofore been so simple."[13]

Earning the Right

His philosophy as an actor was to "earn the right" to play a given role, De Niro biographer John Baxter recounts,[14] and as we'll see, the actor applied that tenet to his first major film role. Transformation was key: to that end, according to

some of his early associates, he concocted various headshots and one composite depicting him in different characterizations, sometimes young, sometimes old.

During this time he received steady encouragement and support from two female actors: Sally Kirkland and Shelley Winters. Kirkland was active in New York's theater scene and made a strong impression on the film screen in Milton Moses Ginsberg's frank sexual psychodrama *Coming Apart* in 1968. In Baxter's book, Kirkland is quoted as describing her early relationship with De Niro: "We were very, very close friends then in that whole time frame. I think he liked me because I had always been very social and he was always shy. I really thought he was a genius and I was always telling people, 'Hire Robert De Niro.'"[15] Together the pair workshopped characters; Kirkland claimed that she helped teach the struggling-with-his-anger young De Niro yoga ("I'm never sure if he practiced it again"[16]). She soon introduced De Niro to Winters, who, though a Hollywood luminary, also served as something of a den mother for the young actors around the various stage scenes and schools of New York. (Winters would later bring De Niro along when Roger Corman and American International Pictures called her out to Hollywood for *Bloody Mama*.)

As the sixties darkened into the seventies, De Niro the actor found himself for the first time in a kind of role he would play for Martin Scorsese— that of a surrogate for a director making films out of a personal vision. De Niro played the role of Jon Rubin in two films directed by De Palma, who was not yet the gleefully perverse technocrat of *Carrie* (1976), *Dressed to Kill* (1980), and other formally advanced thrillers. The low-budget De Palma, while fond of split-screen and other devices, is more noteworthy for a relentlessly sardonic and mordant sensibility that aspires to the condition of satire—an atmosphere in which De Niro does not exactly thrive.

In *Born to Win* (1970), the second feature film directed by Czech filmmaker Ivan Passer and the director's first after immigrating to the US in the late sixties, young De Niro, who had continued to live with his mother during the years of scraping and striving, actually plays a cop—something he wouldn't do again for a rather

De Niro as the not-too-bright catcher Bruce Pearson in *Bang the Drum Slowly*.

long time. His character, Danny, is undercover, with a knit cap and long shaggy hair, and he has the gruff, bluff manner that will be standard issue for cinematic New York cops for years to come— Dennis Franz's detective in De Palma's *Dressed to Kill* is an older, more out-of-shape variation on the theme. The other roles that dot De Niro's early years in film look forward to personages he'd portray in a more prominent way in the future: an imported-from-Italy Mafia cat's-paw in *The Gang That Couldn't Shoot Straight*, the driver of a non-Yellow cab in *Jennifer on My Mind* (1971), a filmmaker in *Sam's Song* (1969).

The baseball player from the Georgia backwoods that De Niro plays in *Bang the Drum Slowly* was, of course, not his first good ole boy. His Lloyd Barker in *Bloody Mama* was a good ole bad boy, and Shelley Winters has been quoted describing how devotedly he crafted his portrayal of Lloyd, whose eventual troubles (aside from being the son of a career criminal obliged to abet her activities) are foreshadowed in the first half hour, in which he's seen huffing glue while building a model airplane, getting goofily stoned, and falling backward in his chair exclaiming "Hallelujah!" The B-movie charge of *Bloody Mama* comes out of the determinedly squalid depiction of the various ailments and dysfunctions of Winters's character and of her brood; one son's an epileptic, another is gay (a taboo in the period in which the film is set, and even, though slightly

less so, in the time it was made), and so on. Within this structure De Niro's attempts to make his junkie half-wit character a credible figure seem largely wasted.

Major League

His work as Bruce Pearson in *Bang the Drum Slowly* is more fleshed-out, and more affecting. *Bang the Drum Slowly* is, among other things, the story of the friendship between the not-too-bright third-string catcher Pearson and pitcher Henry "Author" Wiggen, a friendship that grows deeper once Wiggen learns that Pearson's dying. The piece originated as a novel by Mark Harris. It was subsequently adapted for the screen as a teleplay, written by Arnold Schulman and directed by Daniel Petrie and broadcast on *The United States Steel Hour* (this was back when the line made famous in *The Godfather Part II*, "We're bigger than US Steel, Michael," would really *mean* something). The roles of the ballplayer friends Wiggen and Pearson were played by Paul Newman and Albert Salmi respectively. Salmi, a hulking, looming figure, particularly relative to the lithe, blither Newman, lumbers through the man-child role, applies a childlike sweetness to his line readings of the purposefully goofy dialogue, and leaves it at that, while Newman starts off in glib mode and ends up in glib-but-humbled mode.

Despite the reputation Robert De Niro acquired over the years as an actor's actor, the history of his live theater work is a thin one. Aside from a sole review in a North Carolina newspaper in May 1967 of a traveling production of *Tchin-Tchin*, in which De Niro is singled out for special praise by reviewer Gene S. Key ("he revealed the anguish of a lost soul"[a]), notices of De Niro's early stage work proved elusive during my research for this text. Similarly, biographies and profiles don't provide much in the way of anecdotes about De Niro being an electrifying stage presence. Sally Kirkland was sufficiently impressed by his work in the satirical camp stage play *Glamour, Glory and Gold*, starring Holly Woodlawn and Candy Darling, the drag performers who had achieved notoriety in Andy Warhol's stock company, such as it

was, to befriend the young De Niro in the late sixties. But most of the stories of his power, his ability to disappear into a role, and his dedication stem from those who observed De Niro at Stella Adler's classes, in the Actors Studio, or at an audition. (For his audition for *The Wedding Party*, which was his introduction to director Brian De Palma, De Niro riffed on a rousing speech from Clifford Odets's play *Waiting for Lefty*.) Unlike his contemporaries Al Pacino or Meryl Streep, De Niro chooses not to tune his instrument with regular returns to the stage. He made one such foray, in the late eighties, and unsurprisingly, given his stated lack of comfort with, or even interest in, period roles (contrast this with Pacino's late-period forays into popular Shakespeare scholarship, as in his 1996 film *Looking*

for Richard), he worked in a contemporary drama: twenty-six-year-old Reinaldo Povod's *Cuba and His Teddy Bear*. The play's engagement began at Joseph Papp's Public Theater, but demand soon moved it to Broadway, and the production was sold out for its entire July to September run. According to John Baxter's account, the most galvanic moment in De Niro's performance as a Cuban drug dealer occurred during a confrontation in which he loses his temper at another character who offers drugs to his young son. "De Niro took the 185-pound man by the shirt, lifted him off his feet, and held him against the wall. 'I can't tell you how long he held him,' said Irwin Winkler, 'There is no way you can hold up 185 pounds against a wall like that. It was just the force of the actor doing that. It was remarkable.'"[b]

De Niro was hungry for either lead role in this picture; he initially read for the role of Wiggen. According to Baxter, the actor went through seven auditions, and when he was finally hired, told director John Hancock, "There may be more talented people, but no one will work harder."[17] In the press book for the film issued by its distributor Paramount Pictures, De Niro is quoted saying, "I traveled to Georgia to get the right inflection of words. I talked with the mayor of a small Georgia town that Pearson might have lived in. I looked around at clothing stores and the manner of dress of the people—and I learned how to chew tobacco."

Indeed, on screen De Niro is almost never without a lump in his cheek, and he's depicted consuming so much "chaw" that one wonders how he managed not to become addicted to the stuff in real life—inveterate tobacco chewers will tell you the weed in this form is tougher to kick than any smokable product. De Niro's oral dexterity impressed Jim Bouton, the irreverent major league pitcher turned author (his 1970 road diary–cum–career memoir *Ball Four* scandalized a sport that by this time was just barely hanging on to its false squeaky-clean image), one of the players with whom De Niro consulted on the role: "The best thing De Niro learned was how to talk while chewing tobacco and to spit it out without getting it all over himself, which is something most real ball players have not mastered."[18] De Niro considered more

than speech and idiosyncratic behavior. "I saw in every baseball game how relaxed the players were," he recalled during an AFI symposium that was recorded and printed in *American Film* magazine. "I could pick it up. I could practice in my room watching them do nothing."[19]

Far from Laredo

The opening credits of *Bang the Drum Slowly* are in red, white, and blue, as presumably befits what has almost always been marketed as the all-American sport. Stephen Lawrence's score incorporates themes from "Streets of Laredo," the western ballad from which the title phrase of the movie is derived. The opening shots of the film depict Wiggen and Pearson leaving a building with a sign reading "Mayo Clinic" over its entrance. Michael Moriarty, as Wiggen, speaks in voice-over, introducing Pearson in pro baseball terms: "A million dollars' worth of promise with two cents of delivery." Moriarty strikes a nice balance between the character's self-regard and innate decency and conveys that the character is just a trifle more urbane than pretty much all of his colleagues. (Wiggen is nicknamed "Author" by his teammates, which Pearson misapprehends as "Arthur.") The movie brings the hammer down on Pearson right away: he's gravely ill, and only Wiggen knows it, and Wiggen aims to keep it that way. After a road trip down to Pearson's

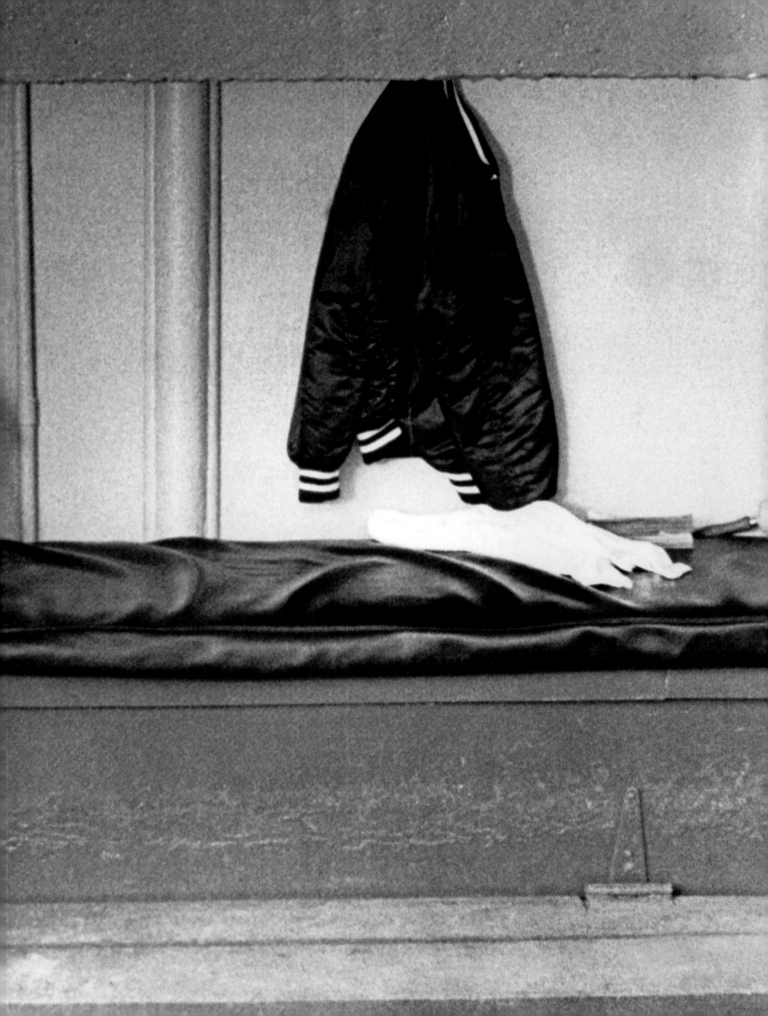

homestead, Bruce assures his people: "Oh, I'm fine; never better."

"I didn't try to play dumb," De Niro told an interviewer at the time of the movie's release.[20] "I just tried to play each scene for where it was. Some people are dumb but they're not dumb—I guess they're insensitive, but they're not insensitive to everything. It's kind of hard to say it. Do you know what I'm getting at?" With his floppy not-quite-pompadour hair, almost ever-smiling eyes, white socks beneath his brown loafers, and chaw-filled mouth frequently agape, his Pearson conveys not insensitivity but a cluelessness that coincides with an absolute openness. While visiting his parents with Wiggen, Pearson asks about a card game that Wiggen and the teammates play with fellow travelers, and win a fair sum of money so doing. Wiggen explains to him that the game's name, "Tegwar," actually stands for "The Exciting Game With No Rules." It's a con in which a couple of ball players beat credulous fans for small amounts by acting as if whatever hand they have beats the hand the opponent shows. Pearson can't grasp the concept; the material is there to persuade the audience that the character's low IQ is a sign of purity. When Pearson's allowed to sit in on a game, De Niro, to his credit, doesn't try to hammer that conceit home; he merely depicts Pearson trying to follow and, most crucially, his joy in sharing the winnings of his buddies.

Because all Pearson finally wants, as Wiggen seems to recognize, is a sense of belonging. "I always been pretty much of a nobody," Pearson complains, but the way De Niro has the character say it, the words come out as plain fact rather than self-pity. When Wiggen consults with the owner of his team, the New York Mammoths, for a contract renegotiation, he insists on an unusual clause that will keep him and Pearson professionally tied, as word around the bullpen suggested Pearson was close to being traded out. No one understands why he's making this demand—"What are you, a couple of fairies or something?" Gardenia's flustered manager taunts, giving a fair example of what passed for gruff quasi-avuncular man-to-man dialogue in certain American pictures of this period. Wiggen's idea is to keep close to Pearson and protect his interests (in a peculiar subplot, a call girl and baseball quasi-groupie is trying to swindle Pearson into making her the beneficiary of his insurance policy), and once Pearson's not-frequently-cited disease (at one point the name "Hodgkin" is mentioned, and that's pretty much it) claims him, that will be that.

"You always had confidence. I never had confidence," Pearson mentions to Wiggen during one of their heart-to-hearts. While Wiggen at first is loath to let anyone know of Pearson's condition (another subplot has Gardenia's manager hiring a detective to track Wiggen and Pearson's movements together in the prior off-season), once

word gets out, the tough, cranky Mammoths are revealed to be a pretty swell bunch of guys after all, and Pearson gets his wish. The team makes them one of theirs, and the club starts playing better.

"They Won't Bite You"

There's a subsequent locker room scene in which Gardenia, again upping the ham quotient, semi-apologizes to Pearson for having been hard on him.

"I, uh, probably ate you out now and then, but never without a reason," he says with sternness and an undercurrent of affection.

De Niro's Pearson, mindful of maintaining the proper attitude toward authority, shakes his head, ready to own up to his inadequacy as a player. "No sir, you only ate me out for doing dumb things …"

"No, no, no, no, I ate you out for the good of the club," Gardenia pontificates, "and for your own pocketbook. Never"—and here Gardenia points his finger and approaches De Niro— "for anything personal"—and here he wags his finger. "Because I know that you know"—and Gardenia points again—"that personally I never had anything but the greatest respect for you as a human being." Which everyone understands to be a complete crock—everyone but Pearson, that is. Only De Niro does not play the response quite that way. When he grins and drawls , "Yes, sir, that was how I always felt," there's a very slight hint of disingenuousness there that almost encourages multiple readings. Is this Pearson making fun of himself? Making fun of the coach? Is it De Niro making fun of the character? Is it De Niro making fun of Gardenia? In a way, the line and the reading are funniest when seen from that last perspective. It's a pretty astonishing moment. Something about what he's doing leaps out in a way that he may not necessarily be controlling.

The aspects of the character and his situation De Niro *is* controlling often yield very affecting results. When Pearson starts waking up with night sweats and once says to Wiggen, "I'm scared. Hold on to me," he has a vulnerability that is almost tactile in its directness. It's not a quality one often associates with De Niro or his characters, but it's something that he brings to bear in his preparation for performance. Decades after *Bang the Drum Slowly*, De Niro played the role of a racist diving instructor in *Men of Honor* (2000), which starred the African-American actor Cuba Gooding Jr. as De Niro's charge. It took De Niro some time to wrap himself around the more unsavory aspects of his character, moving Gooding to observe, "De Niro wears his insecurities on his sleeve. I guess the word is vulnerable. He's a very vulnerable actor. He chooses not to try anything expressive emotionally until he truly believes it. And if that takes rehearsal time, so be it."[21] (One finds hints of this very vulnerability in an interview De Niro

gave to *Scholastic Scope* magazine, a periodical for schoolkids, at the time of *Bang the Drum Slowly*'s release: "Meeting audiences is easy. Meeting people is tough. I have to keep telling myself, 'Go on. Say hello. They won't bite you.'"[22])

De Niro Sings!

As the disease starts to debilitate Pearson, De Niro's physical work in the role grows ever more impressive: the shakiness of his catching stance, the slump in his shoulders, the lack of spring in his step, an ever-encroaching sense of sagging tiredness. All of which mixes with his character's newfound exhilaration in being one of the guys. In one ingratiatingly goofy sequence, Pearson is shown as part of "The Singing Mammoths," a septet of players appearing on local television crooning a country ballad ("Look Before You Weep"). As with the footage of him doing quasi-slapstick in *Greetings*, it's fun to watch (and hear) De Niro singing, uninhibitedly and not all that well, at a point in his career before his image had been codified to a point that "De Niro Sings!" could become a point of interest and intrigue as salient as "Garbo Laughs!" (See chapter nine, on *Meet the Parents*.) "It was a club, like it should've been all year but never was," Wiggen observes of the Mammoths' season at the movie's end. The team is ahead, and soon the gonzo Texan catcher with whom the club was threatening to replace Pearson is entertaining the team during a rainout by singing and playing guitar. He gets to "Streets of Laredo." Some of the teammates think it's in bad taste for him to play that mournful song, and some of them don't. Again, De Niro doesn't play Pearson for a holy fool. He understands that whatever's going on in this disagreement, it's something to do with his benefit, and he's grateful just to be considered: his straightness makes the character moving. After this the movie does not attempt to manipulate the tear ducts of the audience as shamelessly as one was sure it was going to. The Mammoths move to the playoffs, and Pearson moves home, and he's not given a death scene. Instead, we see Wiggen at his funeral, and in voice-over he observes of Pearson, "He wasn't a bad fella. No worse than most, and probably better than some." And he speaks the lesson that the whole experience has taught him: "From here on in, I rag nobody."

Okay then. In 1988, the then-president of the National League, A. Bartlett Giamatti, pronounced *Bang the Drum Slowly* his favorite baseball movie.[23] Given the ethic that Giamatti, father of the actor Paul, tried to promote in baseball (he's the man who insisted on player Pete Rose's permanent ban from the game after gambling violations, in spite of Rose's nearly universal popularity among fans), this is an understandable choice. But for those not concerned by such issues, the movie is not such great shakes, even in its position as a "baseball movie." It's flat-looking, frequently off-kilter dramatically, and inept tonally. It is in no way emblematic of the "New Hollywood" film with which De Niro would become inextricably tied. But it is anchored and in many respects redeemed by its two lead performances, which, by the end of its ninety-six minutes, we're kind of irritated that we haven't seen more of. Moriarty's is at this point in time universally acknowledged as the lesser of the two performances, and that's slightly unfair. His work here is unusually intelligent and alert, and he's respectfully aware of his obligation to give De Niro something real to play off of. Perhaps one reason Salmi's version of Pearson in the teleplay comes off as it does has to do with Newman's enthusiastic hotdogging of the Wiggen role. Moriarty does no such thing. De Niro, by the same token, doesn't take undue advantage of the opportunity Moriarty hands him to run away with the movie. With the exception of the response to Gardenia in the locker room scene, he draws within the lines, but how beautifully he does so. Watching him, one doesn't necessarily see "the new Brando," but he does give every indication of being, as an actor, a very complete package.

The tools are all in place. Now he needs an artist who can use them right. That artist was very close. In fact Martin Scorsese grew up only blocks away from De Niro.

Top: Pearson talks to Wiggen (Michael Moriarty) as he prepares for a "date" with Katie (Ann Wedgeworth).

Center: Pearson, fearing he's dying, asks Wiggen to call the doctor: it's a false alarm.

Bottom: The gauche Pearson is invited to join Wiggen and others in the Singing Mammoths.

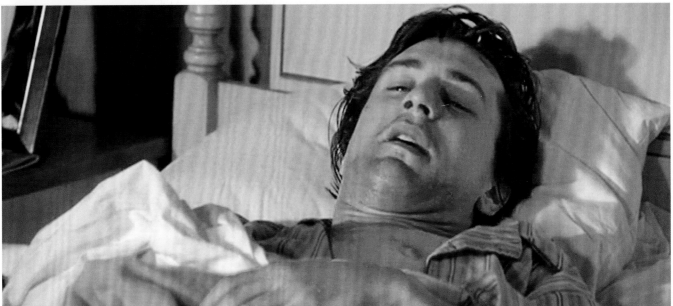

2

Johnny Boy

Mean Streets (1973)
Martin Scorsese

"It's a family thing, it's complicated. I can't explain it, all right?"
—Charlie (Harvey Keitel)

As with *Bang the Drum Slowly*, De Niro approached *Mean Streets* wanting a different role from the one he got. "[M]y recollection is that Marty offered me a choice of any of the four parts, except Harvey Keitel's part, Charlie," De Niro told Lawrence Grobel. "At the time, I felt like I should be asking for the lead. There was a self-worth side of me; I had done a lead in *The Gang That Couldn't Shoot Straight*—which was a total disaster—and I felt like this was a step down. I was thinking, I want to work with Marty, but I'm going to hold out for the lead. Then I ran into Harvey Keitel in the street. He said, 'I think you should do that part.' I said, 'I know, but, to be honest about it, I think I should have the part you have.' I said it in such a way that he wasn't offended by it; I was just being straight about it. He said, 'Well, I think you would do very well with Johnny Boy.' I couldn't see it. But finally, I mulled it over and decided I'd do it."[24]

These professional maneuverings among friendly rivals belie but also underscore the very personal roots of *Mean Streets*, the third feature directed by Martin Scorsese. "I showed *Boxcar Bertha* in a rough cut of about two hours to John Cassavetes. John took me back to his office, looked at me and said, 'Marty, you've just spent a whole year of your life making a piece of shit. It's a good picture, but you're better than the people who make this kind of movie. Don't get hooked into the exploitation market, just try and do something different.' Jay Cocks, who was then the *Time* film critic, had shown him *Who's That Knocking at My Door?* And he had loved it. He said I must go back to making that kind of film and was there anything I had that I was really dying to make. I said, 'Yes, although it needs a rewrite.' 'Well, rewrite it then!'"[25]

The director's two prior fiction features, *Boxcar Bertha* (1972) and *Who's That Knocking at My Door* (1967), were both low-budget pictures for which Scorsese had a finite amount of artistic freedom. As for *Bertha*, it was an assignment from American International Pictures, with Roger Corman producing, and Corman had hoped that it would function as

a sort of sequel to *Bloody Mama* (which, like *Bertha*, is a Depression-era tale of violence), the film in which Robert De Niro played the junkie son of the title character.

A Man and His Hat

Mean Streets, like *I Vitelloni*, Federico Fellini's 1953 picture (and third directorial feature), is the story of young men who are not quite ready to grow up yet. But while Scorsese cites the Fellini picture as an influence, his vision is not nearly as light-hearted. Within the unit that its four protagonists form there's a central duo: Charlie, a largely buttoned-up, slightly glib, but thoroughly tormented soul who's reluctantly learning the ropes as a collector for his minor mobster uncle, and Johnny Boy, a hopped-up, mischievous ne'er-do-well and neighborhood terror who's like a bad baby brother to Charlie. Of the many responsibilities Charlie feels burdened by—his going-nowhere relationship with Teresa (who happens to be a cousin of Johnny's); his desire to please his uncle despite his apprehension that the hood life, even a slightly upscale variant of it, is not for him; his preoccupation with sin and suffering; his concomitant conviction that you do your real penance not in church but "in the streets"—his responsibility for Johnny Boy is the one that weighs the heaviest on him and winds up costing him the most.

After the necessary negotiations to get the movie made, Scorsese cast Harvey Keitel in the role of Charlie, the most directly autobiographical character in the movie. (Early versions of the script had Charlie taking arts classes at a local college—Scorsese himself studied and briefly taught at NYU—but this aspect of the character was jettisoned.) Keitel had played a similar role in *Who's That Knocking at My Door?*, and although Keitel was of Polish extraction and Jewish, his particular brand of volatility, a quality of seeming incredibly withdrawn even when acting in an overtly voluble manner, made him a good fit to stand in for the wiry, wired Scorsese. Scorsese recalls that because of their old neighborhood connection, the part of the firecracker Johnny Boy in *Mean Streets* was "perfect" for De Niro. After the actor accepted the part, Scorsese

De Niro plays the nihilistic Johnny Boy, seen here in a scene near the end of the film pulling a gun on loan shark Mikey.

29

visited him at his apartment on Fourteenth Street, "and he had clothes from the old days. I remember him putting a hat on. And I said to myself, 'Oh, it's perfect!' I didn't tell him that, I just said, 'Oh, it's good, it's good.' But when I saw the hat, I knew it was … him. Just leave him alone, don't touch him."[26]

Four Friends

The hat of which Scorsese speaks may well be the one that De Niro wears as the viewer is introduced to Johnny Boy in *Mean Streets*. After the film's evocative, galvanic opening/ credits sequence, in which Charlie awakes from a nightmare and the movie cuts to the projection of an 8 mm home movie (shots of Little Italy, the feast of San Gennaro, Scorsese's director credit under a shot of Keitel shaking hands with a priest on the steps of a church), accompanied by Phil Spector's production of the Ronettes' classic "Be My Baby," *Mean Streets* gives us quick sketches of its four main characters. Tony (David Proval) is seen trying to run his dive bar in semirespectable fashion, tossing out a junkie he finds shooting up in a men's room stall, upbraiding the regular who sold the scag, then ranting at the ostensible bouncer who's been sitting at the bar doing nothing. Michael (Richard Romanus), standing by some trucks in a parking lot by the East River, has a stance that says he thinks he's a big shot, but he's not that bright; the shipment of goods he hopes to make a black market killing on is not, as he believes, a stock of German lenses. "That's a telescopic one," he boasts to a would-be client as he examines the goods. The fellow Michael wants to make a deal with says "It's not German, it's Jap. This is an adaptor. It's not a lens. You bought two shipments of Jap adaptors, not lenses." Michael mouths the words "Jap adaptors" and rolls his eyes.

Johnny Boy's appearance after these two vignettes is an anarchic whoopee cushion in contrast to the workaday lowlifedom preceding it. Wearing a short leather coat, flared trousers, something like a bowling shirt, and a high-top brown fedora with a satin belt, he saunters up to a mailbox, puts a package in, strolls away. He looks back, he touches his face, he looks back again, he touches his face again, stroking his cheeks with both hands, he picks up speed, runs a bit, and before he can duck into a storefront doorway, the mailbox explodes. He's a little rattled himself, but soon looks upon his work and a grin starts to play on his face, and he runs from the scene in delight. "JOHNNY BOY," the all-caps title in classic old-school typewriter font reads. The final introduction is for Charlie, seen in church, questioning and testing his faith, putting his finger to the flame of a lit candle, bringing everything down to a philosophical minor key.

"It's a Family Thing"

Mean Streets follows Charlie; the movie's perspective is almost entirely in what prose writers call "close third person." But Johnny practically dogs Charlie, like a physical manifestation of his never-not-guilty conscience. After the characters are introduced, we find Charlie in party mode. But Charlie can't even long enjoy his own self-inflicted torment over his crush on one of the female go-go dancers at Tony's bar. Soon Michael shows up with surly questions about when Charlie's friend Johnny Boy is going to pay back some money he owes. "Michael, Michael, nobody's out to screw you! I guarantee that," Charlie says, making a *poof!* hand gesture into the smoky air. A scuffle breaks out near the men, interrupting their increasingly tense discussion. Michael cuts to the chase: "I don't understand why you hang around with a punk kid. I mean, he's the biggest jerkoff around." Charlie's glib façade almost drops completely. "Don't say that, Michael …" Michael pushes again, and Charlie, now suddenly vulnerable, says, "It's a family thing, it's complicated. I can't explain it, all right?" His words pick up speed as he recovers his bearings, his politician's confidence. "But really he's a good kid," he concludes firmly, and Michael chooses to accept that. For now.

Then the "good kid" shows up. Entering from the left side of the frame, a spring in his step, leading two young women, he practically pirouettes, showing off his long wool coat. He's got a long-collared white shirt and a garish tie on now, and that same fedora from when he blew up the mailbox. (The hat now resides in the collection of "Robert De Niro Costumes and Personal Effects" at the Harry Ransom Center of the University of Texas, Austin.) At the coat check he checks his trousers, opening his coat to reveal his boxer shorts beneath his shirt's fly front. The two young women giggle delightedly.

"You talk about penance, and you send this in through the door," Charlie thinks as he watches Johnny put his pants back on. As Johnny walks down the length of the bar in slow motion (this particular brand of which would become something of a Scorsese trademark), his arms draped over each of the girls' shoulders, the soundtrack blares the Rolling Stones' "Jumpin' Jack Flash," in case you missed the point. Throughout all of this, image, sound, and performance sync up in perfect calibration with each other; it's bravura filmmaking that sweeps the viewer up.

De Niro's register in this part of what becomes a darker and darker movie is entirely comic, picaresque. Near-constant grin, fake-formal voice as he introduces Charlie and Tony to his would-be conquests ("I met 'em in the Village," Johnny Boy says; "Bohemian," Tony responds, fake-impressed), elaborate feints as he reaches into his wallet to pay for his drinks. Seeing the money, Charlie decides

he has to school Johnny Boy with respect to his obligations, and takes him in the back, despite the risk, dire to Johnny Boy, that they'll lose the girls.

Their exchange, during which Johnny lies his ass off, could have come out of classic-era Abbott and Costello, with more profanity and more at stake, and as we'll see, the filmmakers were entirely aware of this. Once in the back room, the question is put forward: When did Johnny last pay Michael? "*Last* Tuesday?" says Johnny. "Yeah, that's the Tuesday that was last week that's before the one that's about to come up." "My mistake, I'm sorry, forgive me, it was last week, the week before that I was thinking of." And all the while the two smirk at each other, as if they are in fact aware of enacting a kind of comic routine. It's the kind of ease within a certain mode of self-consciousness that's a hallmark of male friendship, particularly in urban environments. But there's also a real sense of each character setting up the other for a fall, even if neither of them consciously knows it … yet.

"The scene in the back room with De Niro and Keitel after they meet in the bar, I thought it would be fun to improvise and show more of the characters. We realized that we liked Abbott and Costello a great deal, their language routines with inverted word-meanings done with wonderful timing," Scorsese recalled. "We tried to keep as much of that as possible […]. The scene was Bob's idea, and since he and Harvey are not afraid to

try things, I said 'Why not?' When I shot it, it was about fifteen minutes long, hilarious and clarified everything totally. It's like the betrayals of trust, one character taking advantage of the other, that I enjoy in the Hope and Crosby movies."[27]

Truth to tell, because Scorsese is a great cinematic artist who also, particularly at this time, overtly disdained what he called "plot," the clarity he speaks of is not wholly present in the Johnny Boy/Charlie relationship. What the trust is, where it comes from, is not really spelled out for the viewer. We know that Charlie's sometime girlfriend Teresa is Johnny Boy's cousin; the other nodes by which they're connected are mostly implied. I wrote in the introduction that De Niro's character in this film barely exists in relation to other people at all. That is, he never is depicted as having anything like a genuine interaction with anybody; he is a constant antagonizing agent, and sometimes the antagonism is amusing, but all he's ever seen revealing of himself is his irritating side. He's a lost soul, but he doesn't seem to care about that; his mischief is what keeps him alive.

Darkening Mischief

As the film goes on, the quality of that mischief is seen coarsening, and it's in this respect that the calibrations of De Niro's performance pay off great dividends. The scene, in the middle of the first half of the film, in which Charlie and his crew go to a

pool hall to straighten out a "misunderstanding"
over an unpaid number should show Charlie at
his politically smoothest ("Saint Charles is here,"
exclaims the rotund pool hall owner, Joey, played
by George Memmoli, as Keitel enters). But Johnny
Boy throws a monkey wrench in the works for no
good reason. No reason at all, really. As Charlie
gets to the payoff, Johnny Boy stage-whispers
that Joey is a "scumbag," and Charlie smoothes
that over. As Joey pours shots at the cash register,
Johnny Boy shakes his head in dissatisfaction. His
initial manner is just a few micrometers to the left
of the bluff and cheerful figure with his pants off
in the first bar scene, but as the scene continues
De Niro pushes it into nonsensical nasty self-
righteous arrogance and turf-calling provocation,
complaining to Joey to turn down the volume on
the jukebox because it's giving him a headache.
"Hey, the girls like the music loud," Joey says
with a shrug. "Girls? You call those skanks girls?"
Johnny Boy shoots back, setting the stage for the
standard you-gonna-let-him-talk-to-me-like-that
overture to a physical fight. (The comedy does
not entirely dissipate, as the subsequent exchange
introduced the term "mook" into the semipopular
lexicon.) None of it is even vaguely necessary, and
in the aftermath the guys are still laughing, but
there's a distinct sense of a line having been crossed.

The tension hangs over the movie like a pall
even in the scenes in which De Niro doesn't
appear or is not the central focus, and worse

and worse things keep happening. A drunk is
shot to death in the men's room by an assassin
who, in a theatrical flourish, pulls his hippie-
long hair from under his coat before plugging
his victim in the back. (The assassin and victim
are played by Robert and David Carradine,
respectively; Scorsese worked with brother David
on *Boxcar Bertha*.) A Vietnam vet freaks out at
his homecoming party at Tony's, after Charlie's
epic drunk (conveyed via a traveling shot that
anticipates Spike Lee's notorious disembodied-
walking shots and that is scored to the novelty
tune "Rubber Biscuit," which never sounded more
sickly) at that party. Teresa suffers a bad epileptic
seizure in a stairwell. All the while Johnny Boy's
debt to Michael grows. ("Twenty dollars doesn't
pay the interest for two hours," Michael tells
Charlie when Charlie offers him some cash. "Now
with the vig it's almost three thousand.") And all
Johnny Boy can do is stand on a rooftop firing
a gun at a clothesline belonging to a woman he
hates "with a passion."

These events wind up playing like omens,
which casts light on the fact that early on the
script was titled *Season of the Witch*. In one
conversation Charlie says he'd like to open a
bar and call it by that name. The title *Mean
Streets* was taken from Raymond Chandler, and
Scorsese says that some Little Italy denizens took
exception to a movie of that title shooting in their
neighborhood.

"The Only Jerkoff Around Here That I Can Borrow Money From"

The tension breaks with De Niro's most bravura piece of acting in the film. "I got nothing," Johnny Boy protests to Charlie after the two fight, for real this time (previously we saw them horsing around with garbage pail lids, another bit of improv from Keitel and De Niro). Out of options, Johnny Boy has visited Charlie's mobster uncle, who's already reprimanded Charlie about his relationship with Johnny. Now he's got to show up for Michael, who's already hired an enforcer of sorts (a hood Charlie calls "Shorty," played by Scorsese himself; he said in 1974 that casting himself saved money and admitted he was also keen to handle a gun on film[28]) and who will not be pleased at Johnny Boy's lack of funds. Waxing repentant and fatalistic for Charlie, he completely changes his attitude once Michael shows up at Tony's. Standing behind the bar, fake-apologizing to Michael for keeping him waiting, he has the same grin, the same syncopated, quick manner of speech, as he displayed in his initial conquering-hero, court-jester stance at the bar. But there's been a fundamental shift. The imp is now a full-blown nihilist. "You know something, Mikey? You make me laugh, you know that? You know, I borrow money all over this neighborhood, left and right, from every body"—De Niro pronounces "everybody" as two words, giving special stress to "body," as if turning a screw. "I never pay them back, so I can't borrow no money from no body no more, right? So who does that leave me to borrow money from but you? I borrow money from you because you're the only jerkoff around here"—and here he grins, very wide—"that I can borrow money from without paying back." He holds a ten-dollar bill in his hand and puts a lighter to it. "Because, you know, that's what you are. That's what I think of you. A jerkoff."

Scorsese says, "We did the climactic scene where Bobby suddenly pulls a gun on Richard Romanus on the next to last day of shooting. Something had happened between Bobby and Richard that was real, and I played on it."[29] According to Romanus, "In the scene where Bobby insults me, where he tells me I was stupid to lend him money in the first place, I started to laugh. Bobby got angry. He thought I should be angry, which I was, but by laughing I was saving face. He thought I should be fuming but he had no control over my reactions. Sometimes the reaction you get from your acting partner is not the reaction you want. Then you simply have to react off that."[30]

As riveting as De Niro is, the reactions of the other actors/characters are fascinating, too. Everybody knows that it's all over but the shooting, as it were. Charlie can't believe what's happening, while Proval's Tony acts almost like a sidekick to Johnny Boy at the beginning of his

If it's not clear in 1968's *Greetings*, in which the three young white male characters trying to dodge the draft are treated by director and coscreenwriter Brian De Palma as a unit, *Hi, Mom!*, De Palma's subsequent feature from 1970 creates the distinct impression that the character Jon Rubin, played in both films by De Niro, is meant to be the director's stand in. Quiet and bookish but also highly sardonic, Rubin discovers the joys of voyeurism in the first film and channels that kink into a meager profession in the pornographic film business in the second.

The fit is awkward, and it's hard to figure out just where the fault lies. Both director and actor were relative novices at the time. In subsequent films the voyeurs De Palma put in dangerous situations were deliberately less sophisticated versions of himself, e.g., the high-school science whiz who helps solve his mom's murder in *Dressed to Kill* (1980), the streetwise soundman (played by John Travolta, another actor who got his start nailing urban characters) of *Blow Out* (1981), the betrayal-addled actor who descends into the pornographic underworld in *Body Double* (1984). (It is worth noting that the scene in which Craig Wasson's character in the latter film walks in on his girlfriend while she's having enthusiastic sex with another man is practically a clone of a similar scene in *Hi, Mom!*) While De Niro is entirely game for everything the part calls for with respect to actual enactment, there's a noticeable hesitation in much of his work, as if he's processing the character while acting him. De Niro would have no such problem the next and, up to this point, last time he worked with De Palma, conjuring an ever-enraged and brisk Al Capone in the director's pulp extrapolation *The Untouchables* (1987).

With Martin Scorsese he found a more comfortable fit, perhaps because they shared a more direct affinity, perhaps because the characters in which De Niro functioned as Scorsese's surrogate operate far from the circumstances of filmmaking and embody the destructive emotions rather than aspire to specific characteristics of each man, urban identities notwithstanding. The loneliness of Travis Bickle, the irresolvable anger of La Motta, the neurotic fame-hunger of Rupert Pupkin: De Niro can be the instrument for all of this because, regardless of whether he'll come out and say it the way Scorsese does, they are or have been a part of him as well.

monologue, raising his eyebrows after a particular zinger. As Johnny Boy sets fire to the bill, he makes his final declaration of principles: "And I'll tell you something else, Mikey. I fuck you right where you breathe, 'cause I don't give two shits about you or nobody else."

Pre-Punk Pose

Johnny is putting the last nail in his coffin, and he follows this with one more gesture of bravado, the pulling of the gun, which Michael says Johnny doesn't have "the guts" to use. This is what one could conceivably call "very punk rock." It is likely a complete coincidence that the debut album by the proto-punk band the New York Dolls was released only a few months before *Mean Streets* hit theaters. But one doesn't have to look too far beneath the big hair and the glitter-rock trappings to see the don't-give-a-fuck affinity between Johnny Thunders (born John Anthony Genzale Jr., in Queens), that band's guitarist, and De Niro's Johnny Boy. The pre-punk affinity is prophesied more clearly, and threateningly, in Travis Bickle's mohawk in *Taxi Driver*. By that time Thunders had ditched the Dolls and formed his own Heartbreakers, whose anti-anthemic "Born to Lose" could have served as Johnny Boy's theme music just as aptly as "Jumpin' Jack Flash." In Jim Jarmusch's 1984 *Stranger Than Paradise*, the goofball Lower East

Sider protagonists, played by Richard Edson (onetime drummer for Sonic Youth) and John Lurie (founder of "fake jazz" combo The Lounge Lizards) both sport cheap imitations of Johnny Boy's hat. The image of Johnny Boy grinning as he points the gun was reproduced so many times, in so many contexts, it became a part not just of the iconography of cinema but of New York City itself during this period.

The last we see of Johnny Boy he is staggering out of an alleyway, holding his hand to his neck, trying to stop it from bleeding; Michael has extracted his payment by having "Shorty" shoot him from a moving car, into the moving car in which Charlie, Teresa, and Johnny Boy are trying to escape from the city. As a cop car pulls into the frame, Johnny Boy, a poignant figure for the first time, collapses. We don't know whether he's going to live or die. But he has left a mark.

3

Vito Corleone

The Godfather Part II (1974)
Francis Ford Coppola

"I make him an offer he don't refuse. Don't worry."
—Vito Corleone

De Niro has never made a film with Steven Spielberg or George Lucas, but he worked extensively with two of the most prominent directors who were sometimes called the "movie brats" of seventies Hollywood filmmaking: Martin Scorsese and Brian De Palma. While Coppola is only seven years older than the youngest of this bunch, Spielberg, he was a sort of, if you will, godfather to these other directors. After attending UCLA, he began working in movies while barely out of his teens, doing the semistandard apprenticeship in exploitation before meeting up and allying himself with Roger Corman. Only about twenty-four when he directed his first "real" movie, a low-budget horror picture titled *Dementia 13* (1963), he followed that with *You're A Big Boy Now* (1966), which set a small precedent for the kind of semiautobiographical bildungsroman pictures that De Palma and Scorsese would make at the end of the sixties and in the early seventies, respectively. (These were *Greetings* and *Hi, Mom!* for De Palma and *Mean Streets* for Scorsese, all three starring De Niro.) Coppola came of age in a Hollywood, and a waning studio system, that didn't yet place much value on the wunderkind, so he became a kind of jack-of-all-trades, banking up work until he got opportunities to do more personal projects (see his striking 1969 drama *The Rain People*), and in the meantime friendship-mentoring younger filmmakers such as Lucas.

Coppola was the first of this group of directors to hit the commercial jackpot, and he did so while also hitting an artistic one. It would not be an understatement to say that nobody was expecting *The Godfather* (1972), adapted from a best-selling novel by Mario Puzo, to become a culture-defining smash hit. While Puzo's book had indeed been a best seller, there was a general feeling in Hollywood that gangster pictures were worse than passé, and most of the people going ahead with *The Godfather* didn't anticipate a picture much better than the not-terribly-artistically-reputable *The Brotherhood* (1968). "Sicilian mobster films don't play," then–Paramount

honcho and *Godfather* producer Robert Evans recalls an exhibitor pooh-poohing him while the first movie was in development.[31] Evans had a passion for the project, and a few bad ideas for it: he wanted Alain Delon for the role of Michael. While an indisputable screen icon, Delon is a very specifically limited actor and not a terribly commanding speaker of the English language. Coppola threw himself into this directing assignment with a will and persuaded Evans to roll over and accept Al Pacino for the role of Michael Corleone. This was only one of his many casting coups.

Brando: The First Don

The biggest coup was getting approval to hire Marlon Brando, still an acting legend to some, but to studio-head types a pain-in-the-ass near has-been who, as far as they were concerned, could spend the rest of his career languishing in perverse quasi-exploitation fare such as the super-queasy kidnapping "thriller" *The Night of the Following Day* (1968) and the Michael Winner–directed *Turn of the Screw* prequel *The Nightcomers* (1971), in which Peter Quint (played by Brando) was revealed to have been into bondage. Not yet quite forty, Brando got the role of the patriarch Vito Corleone, whose age is not given in the film but whose provenance is, in a word, old.

Brando made a comeback out of it, approaching the role with a combination of Method devotion (getting a mouthpiece to alter the shape of his cheeks, creating a distinctive manner of speech, putting a damper on his still not-entirely-inconsiderable sexual smolder) and eccentric nonchalance (he read much of his dialogue off of cue cards strategically placed on the set). More than a comeback, Brando's performance was heralded as definitive in American cinema and stands as pretty much the axiom of not only gangster cinema but also a particular misapprehension of the gangster ethic as defined in popular culture: the chimera of the "man of respect" who is in reality pretty much nothing more than a common murderer. Of course the whole appeal of *The Godfather* itself has to do with the varying tensions that exist between the family man and the businessman and the vicious criminal who are all the same person.

Robert De Niro as a younger Vito Corleone in *The Godfather Part II*, the flashback scenes that form a prequel to the original *Godfather* film.

The Next Godfather

By making *The Godfather* a masterpiece, Coppola established himself as a world-class director, but he also succeeded in a way, he insists to this day, he was not interested in doing. At the beginning of the commentary track for the home video version of *The Godfather Part II*, Coppola notes that prior to his beginning to work on it, the movie "didn't exist in any form for me, just the idea that Paramount was interested in doing a sequel." And after Coppola said yes, one of the first things he hooked on to when concocting a story was "to use the material in the original *Godfather* book that dealt with Vito Corleone, his days in Sicily, through his coming to America and becoming the character played by Marlon Brando."

The casting of then-just-thirty-year-old De Niro as young Vito Corleone seemed a much more straightforward matter than the other labyrinthine maneuverings that resulted in the sequel. When Coppola was circling around the project, he initially wanted to serve as producer and to hire Scorsese to direct. Evans refused flat out. But by this point in time it was clear that De Niro was just as much a member of an up-and-coming generation of exciting young actors as Pacino was (we may recall that De Niro fell into a role in the mob send-up *The Gang That Couldn't Shoot Straight* when Pacino pulled out of that picture to make *The Godfather*). It seemed of more concern to critics and other outside observers that De Niro had been hired, for all intents and purposes, to play a young Marlon Brando.

Was that genuinely the case? (In the audio commentary for the video of the film, Coppola recounts, "Of course in my mind I had no assurance that Robert De Niro was really gonna work out in this audacious casting idea, to have some young contemporary actor portray Marlon Brando at an equivalent age. It's one thing now that the film is kind of a classic and older to say 'Oh, yeah, Bobby De Niro was fine,' but at that time it was a risky thing.") For all the similarities they share in performance intensity, De Niro and Brando do not look alike. Nor, as noted before, is De Niro a performer who puts a lot forward in terms of smoldering sexuality. For this role these factors didn't really matter. The last thing we think of Brando's Vito Corleone as being is sexual, and Brando, of course, altered his own appearance significantly for the role.

For all that, on accepting the part, De Niro did have concerns about measuring up to an acting idol. "Preparing to play Vito, De Niro worried that he would be reduced to simply aping Brando's performance," John Baxter writes in his biography of the actor. "He confided his fears to a friend of Brando's, who passed them on. 'I can understand how he would want to do that,' said Brando smugly, 'but he won't be able to.' Finally,

De Niro decided not to try too hard. He dutifully screened *The Godfather* repeatedly—supposedly fifty times. He practiced Brando's habit of lightly touching his left cheek with the tips of his fingers, and developed a version of Brando's rasping voice."[32] Later, talking to Grobel, De Niro said, "I wasn't intimidated [by Brando's precedent]. I just looked at it like a mathematical problem: Brando had already established the character, so I just figured out how to connect to what he had done. We videoed scenes from the movie with a little camera, and I'd play those back, look at them and see what I could do to connect it all."[33]

De Niro was also required to learn enough Sicilian to credibly speak dialogue in that dialect of Italian, which itself contains many subdialects. Finally, he went to the dentist who had fitted Brando with a jowl-accentuating mouthpiece, and had a smaller one made for himself.

"Dumb-witted, Weak, Couldn't Hurt Anyone"

De Niro's performance as young Vito Corleone in New York and Sicily in the early part of the twentieth century is a quiet one containing resonances drawn from what the prior film had already achieved, and adding new ones that bounce back within this film, an epic of three hours and twenty minutes. They even bounce back into the first picture. It's utterly extraordinary, but looking at it, you can understand what De Niro meant about approaching young Vito and his relation to Brando as a mathematical problem. There's no postmodern winking at the audience here. As much as De Niro may or may not have been looking at the prior portrayal of Vito Corleone and thinking of the Marlon Brando he had seen in movie theaters as a kid, the Marlon Brando he wanted to be like, it's clear throughout his performance that he conceives and performs Vito Corleone as a person/character.

The movie introduces Vito as a little boy, only nine years old, and shows us his mother pleading with the local don, Ciccio, not to kill the kid, whose father has been murdered for a slight and his brother for seeking revenge. In this Sicily, vendetta is a way of life, and Ciccio knows when the kid grows up he'll be compelled to seek and take his own revenge. The mother insists that's not possible: "Vito is only nine. And dumb-witted … He's weak. He couldn't hurt anyone," she pleads, in full hearing of her son. As played by moon-eyed Oreste Baldini, that could indeed be the case. Of course, the kid turns out to be not entirely dumb-witted; when his mother tells him to run, he runs, and he barely looks back when one of Ciccio's men blasts her with a shotgun. He doesn't stop running until he reaches Ellis Island, where he's quarantined for smallpox and officials give him for a last name the name of the town, Corleone, that he's running from.

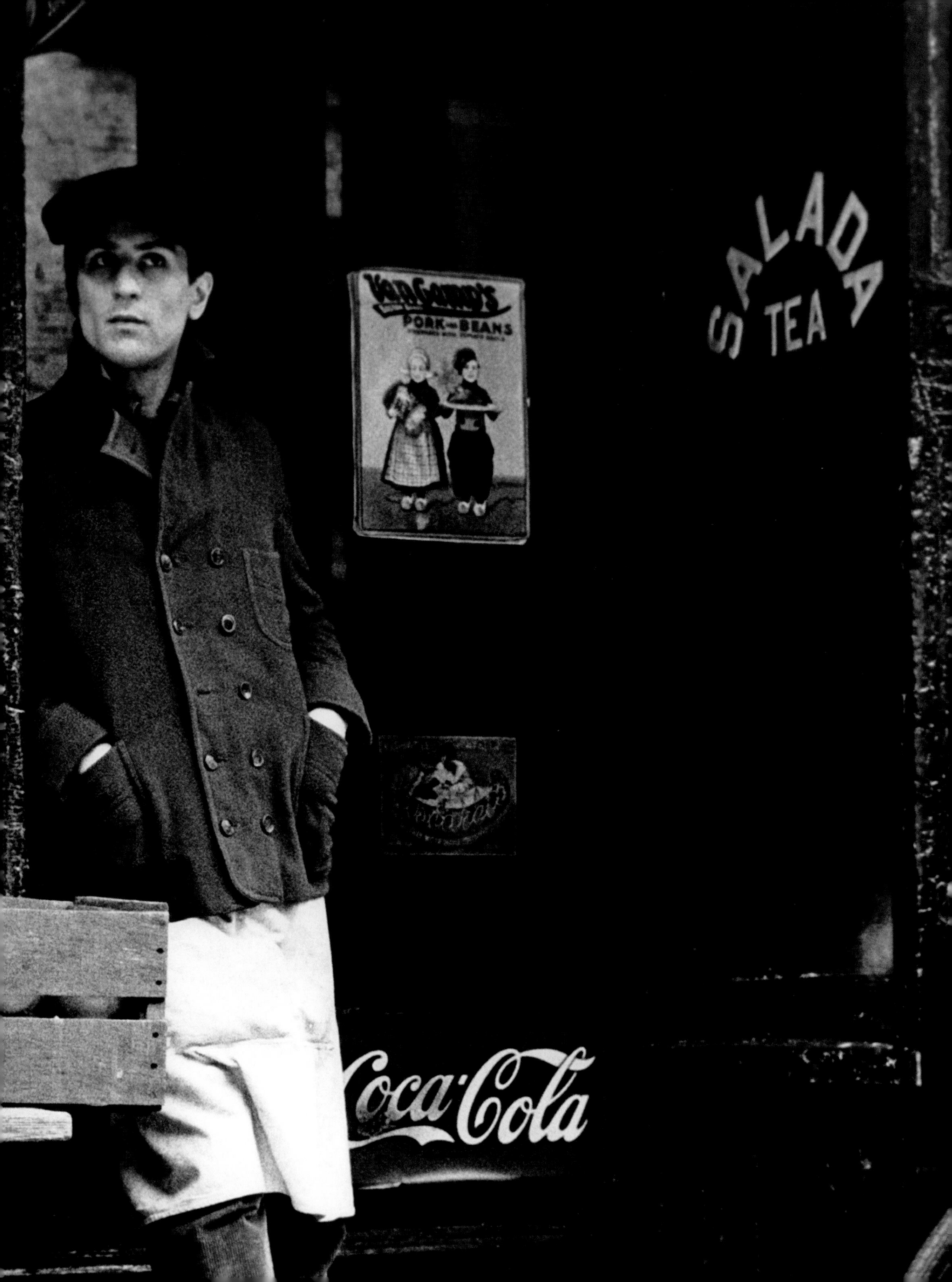
SALADA
TEA
Coca-Cola

Opposite top: Vito is invited to the theater by his friend Genco (Frank Sivero) to see the girl Genco is in love with.

Opposite bottom: Vito at his place of work shortly before his employer is forced to give his job to the nephew of local Mafia boss Fanucci.

Corleone with young Clemenza (Bruno Kirby), for whom he's been hiding guns.

"The Whole Neighborhood Pays Him"

Part of the genius of De Niro's performance—he makes his first appearance about forty-five minutes into the movie, gaunt and clearly not prosperous, but dignified and very clean—is that for a little while he lets you believe what of course is not possible, which is that his character really *is* slow-witted. It's a canny strategy for many reasons, but it's tempting to think that there's also a bit of a private joke on De Niro's part at work here. Producer Fred Roos recalls that at the time De Niro was cast, to have him playing the Don in his early life seemed like "a crazy idea because he had made movies where he played dimwits, like *Bang the Drum Slowly*."[34]

Vito Corleone is not the main player in the first scene in which he ventures outside of his modest New York home. His friend Genco is bringing him to the theater, to lay eyes on a beautiful girl Genco's in love with. (Different forms of theater figure throughout the second two *Godfather* films; the scene of Genco and young Vito watching an operetta—which contains an aria written by Coppola's grandfather; much of the detail in the young Vito sequences stem from the director's family lore—is perverted later on when Michael, Fredo, and company witness a pornographic nightclub show in Havana.) The bushy-eyed Genco is all "wait till you see her," while De Niro's Vito is impassive, and it's soon established that he's a married man in a very serious sense, so that even the thought of what he'd be inclined to think if he weren't married wouldn't occur to him. He wants to be encouraging and supportive of his pal, and that's it. Once they approach the backstage area, and they witness the neighborhood boss Fanucci threatening the theater owner and drooling over the object of Genco's affections—she's the owner's daughter—the quality of Vito's attention changes. Here and in many other subsequent scenes, he watches like the proverbial hawk. On being apprised of just who Fanucci is—he's "with the Black Hand. The whole neighborhood pays him," Genco says, in a voice full of fear—Vito tilts his head back, thinks. It's presumed that Corleone has lived in this neighborhood under these circumstances for years, but this and succeeding scenes contrive to give him an education in how things work where he lives, what the power structure consists of. And what the weapons for overturning the power structure are.

Soon Bruno Kirby turns up as the young version of Clemenza, the hefty hitman of the first *Godfather* picture who gave the immortal instruction to "leave the gun, take the cannoli," and whose impromptu instructions for making tomato sauce are still controversial today. Speaking from one tenement window into another, Clemenza asks Corleone if he can

watch something for him; it's a stash of guns.
(Bruno Kirby, an actor better known for comic
roles—he had a memorable bit in *This Is Spinal
Tap* [1984] and was a foil for Billy Crystal in
When Harry Met Sally [1989] and *City Slickers*
[1991]—is a perfect, measured match for De
Niro. He bluffed his way into the role, telling
Coppola he spoke Sicilian when he didn't.[35] He
had played the son of Richard Castellano, the
actor who portrayed Clemenza, in a sitcom,
though, and had a thorough knowledge of
that actor's bearings.) Taking the guns to the
bathtub, De Niro's Corleone looks at them
with a grave expression on his face. While any
suspicions that he's slow-witted have dissolved
by now, De Niro shows us the gears turning with
careful deliberation.

Once he's decided what to do, he sits down
with Clemenza and the younger version of
Tessio, the character played by Abe Vigoda
in the first film (here the role is John Aprea's)
and lays out his strategy, throwing English-
language phrases into his Sicilian. "I take care of
everything," he assures his friends, promising an
end to Fanucci's reign.

It's here, too, that one notices that as precise
as De Niro's performance is, he does not imbue
it with a fussy consistency but rather puts
a canny strategy to work with respect to the
characteristics of Vito he's emphasizing. So
it's in this scene that the raspiness of the voice,

and the correspondence to the speech patterns
Brando had in the first movie, are at their most
pronounced. On the audio commentary of the
movie's DVD, Coppola, observing this scene,
marvels, "This was one of Bobby De Niro's first
big dialogue scenes, and he had worked on it
so hard, and he had gotten his Sicilian down so
perfectly. We shot these scenes in little sets in
LA, as I recall; this was not even in New York."
Coppola then goes on to observe, "There's a
wonderful thing that Mario [Puzo] does in his
movies, where he has this speech, where you give
people instructions, like 'Tomorrow you go to
the white building. The doorman will come up
to you. He may wink to you. If he does, he is the
one that's going to be your enemy.' So it kind
of predicts what's gonna happen, and then you
sit there and you get to see whether it happens
or not, and that's suspenseful."

It's clear in his delivery of the speech that
De Niro is fully aware of that function of the
dialogue and that his stresses serve that as much
as they serve the development of the character.
As confident as Vito makes himself as he creates
the opportunities to take power, there are
moments on the way up that startle him, such
as, for example, when the towel he's wrapped
around the handgun he assaults Fanucci with
catches fire. As he shakes the flame out, we see
him almost awed at the weapon's—and his
own—force.

Echoes

The scenes in which young Corleone learns the way of crime, sets up the Genco Olive Oil Import Company, and returns to his homeland to exact his revenge on Ciccio (implacably gutting the old man like a pig) take up only forty-five of the 200 minutes of running time of this movie, but such is the power of De Niro's performance that the intelligence and ruthlessness of the character hangs, sometimes like a pall, over the proceedings that occur in the '50s scenes in which son Michael Corleone builds his empire and ironically destroys the family his father thought he was protecting. (After he kills Fanucci, Vito rejoins the crowd celebrating a Catholic feast day and gathers his wife and children on the stoop, and holds baby Michael. "Bob Towne thought this was a great moment," Coppola says on the DVD commentary; "He's whispering to his baby that I've done this for you. And then you realize that the son grows up and he's a murderer too. Maybe it is a good line, I don't know.")

In one exchange with consigliere Tom Hagen (Robert Duvall), Pacino's Michael, fire in his eyes, avers, "All our people are business men, their loyalty is based on that. Now, one thing that I learned from Pop was to try to think as people around you think." And with that line the viewer almost can't help but reflect on De Niro's character and the attention he pays to what's going on around him. When Michael, in one of the few moments of the film in which he seems to be plagued by a conscience, asks his mother, "What did Papa think … deep in his heart? He was being strong… strong for his family. But by being strong for his family, could he lose it?" one can't help but see that young family on the stoop.

Of course all these resonances come about through the filmmaking, not just the performance. As sharp and detailed as De Niro's performance is (and the physicality of it is often startling: Vito's loose, swinging gait as he crosses a street in a rare carefree moment, his strong diffidence as he stands with his hands in his jacket pockets watching others negotiate), the way in which Coppola and the film's three editors weave it into the larger narrative is remarkable. (The early-twentieth-century episodes are almost uniform in length, none longer than fifteen minutes. This had not been Coppola's wish, as it happens, and some of this footage was added to Coppola's so-called *Complete Novel For Television* version of the film.)

A "Family" Classic

The reception for *The Godfather Part II* was close to ecstatic. To this day it is frequently cited as the rare sequel that is not just the equal of but perhaps a better film than its precursor. The movie was nominated for eleven Academy Awards but

De Niro and Pacino

Robert De Niro and Al Pacino first met in the late 1960s, when both actors were struggling to establish themselves. It was through the influence of Pacino and Shelley Winters that De Niro made the lateral move from Stella Adler's Studio of Acting to Lee Strasberg's Actors Studio (which had been cofounded by Elia Kazan, who'd later direct De Niro in *The Last Tycoon* but would never record a professional collaboration with Pacino). The performers competed for parts. De Niro auditioned for the lead in the addiction-themed *The Panic in Needle Park* (1971), which went to Pacino. When Pacino succeeded in getting out of his commitment to perform the comic role of Mario in *The Gang That Couldn't Shoot Straight* so that he could act in *The Godfather*, that part went to De Niro.

It was much remarked at the time of *The Godfather Part II* that it was slightly ironic that the two most electrifying young actors of the time would costar in the same film without having any scenes together, De Niro playing the Mafia kingpin Vito Corleone as a young, relatively uncomplicated man in the early part of the twentieth century and Pacino playing the roiling, ruthless, Shakespearean son of Vito, Michael, in the post–World War II boom of capital and corruption in the United States. Yet in their way, the characters appear to play against each other. This epic not-quite-pairing set an ideal stage for whichever filmmaker would be smart enough, and have sufficient resources, to actually put them in a frame together. Twenty years after *The Godfather Part II*, the filmmaker turned out to be

Michael Mann, for his movie *Heat* (1995). In a slighter, incidental irony, Mann cast the New York–associated actors—Pacino playing a harried cop, De Niro playing a steely thief—in a crime epic set in Los Angeles. And Mann is canny enough to keep the two actors apart, teasing the audience until what has become an iconic scene, an hour and a half into the nearly three-hour movie. Their meeting begins with Pacino's Vincent Hanna pulling over De Niro's Neil McCauley and, because he actually can't run McCauley in on a charge, asking him, "What do you say I buy you a cup of coffee?" De Niro looks the man outside of his car up and down, and after giving the matter serious consideration, says, "Yeah, sure, let's go." It's one of those great De Niro moments in which the way he speaks a mere four words tells the viewer volumes about the character and how he perceives not just the immediate situation but also everything that's led up to that situation. The following diner exchange is a classic for the simple reason that it's better experienced than described. Mann's coup is that he and his film get everything out of the exchange that fans of the actors wanted and hoped for. Years later, show business as usual put the actors together again in *Righteous Kill* (2008), a genre picture that practically seemed like it was nothing special by design.

Is the devil a gangster? De Niro plays him (Louis Cyphre is the character's name, and he sends the titular detective Harry Angel to hell at the end) that way in *Angel Heart* (1986), the overblown supernatural thriller directed by Alan Parker. In this case, he's a very suave gangster, a man of wealth and taste, so to speak, prone to florid metaphors, never raising his voice.

De Niro's Al Capone in Brian De Palma's *The Untouchables* (1987) is a different matter. Sentimental (he cries at the opera), boisterous, prone to rages in which he either rants his most awful wishes (discussing his lawman rival Eliot Ness, he muses, "I want him dead! I want his family dead! I want his house burnt to the ground! I wanna go there in the middle of the night, and I wanna piss on his ashes!") or breaks open the heads of his confederates with a baseball bat.

In Michael Mann's *Heat*, as master thief Neil McCauley, De Niro plays the criminal as a cold-blooded technocrat with a hollow feeling inside, not unlike the title character played by James Caan in Mann's earlier picture *Thief* (1981). Critics who complain that De Niro can't play "smart" don't take this picture into sufficient account, but it is worth considering that De Niro's most compelling portrait of cerebration takes place within a character that lives outside the law.

It all goes back, of course, to his portrayal of Vito Corleone in *The Godfather Part II*. (Contrary to popular misconception, he doesn't exactly play a mafioso in the 1970 *The Gang That Couldn't Shoot Straight*; rather, his Mario is a hotshot bicyclist imported from Italy to be a cat's-paw in a mobster-rigged race, and he's actually one of the freshest things in the stale movie.) Speaking to a reporter in 1973 as he prepared for the role, he allowed, "The character in *The Godfather* is a tricky one. There's a peasant shrewdness, which I haven't found yet. I have to find a bridge between the Brando character and the Pacino character."[c] The operative phrase there is "peasant shrewdness." One gets the impression that mere shrewdness isn't enough to be of interest to the actor. Something specifically contrary, to counter the intelligence, has to be in the mix and complicate the challenge of the character. A law-abiding smart fellow just isn't as interesting.

Vito about to finally take
revenge on Don Francesco
(Giuseppe Sillato), the Sicilian
boss who killed his brother
and mother.

it would have been able to win only nine, because
three of those eleven nominations were in the
same category: Best Supporting Actor. De Niro, of
course, was one nominee; the others were Michael
Gazzo, who played the loyalty-torn Frankie
Pentangeli, and Actors Studio guru Lee Strasberg,
who was making only his second film appearance,
as Meyer-Lansky-based mobster/moneyman
Hyman Roth. De Niro wound up winning the
award but wasn't there to accept it. This was an era
when the vogue was for actors not to show up for
the Oscars; Dustin Hoffman, nominated for Best
Actor that year for Bob Fosse's *Lenny*, pronounced
the Academy Awards "obscene, dirty, and no better
than a beauty contest," and gave his tickets to his
parents.[36] But De Niro's no-show wasn't a protest
but rather a token of his actorly devotion: he was
in Italy, working with Bernardo Bertolucci on a
film. Coppola accepted on his behalf: "I'm happy
one of my boys made it. I think Robert De Niro is
an extraordinary actor and he's going to enrich the
films that will be made in the years to come."[37]

As much as Coppola appreciated De Niro's
devotion and craft, and his contribution to the
work, the actor's singular focus on the work gave
him pause. "I like Bob. I just don't know if he likes
himself," the director later observed. Lawrence
Grobel presented that quote to De Niro during
their late '80s interview, and records De Niro
pausing before responding, "That's an interesting
thing to say. Sometimes I do wish I was a little

happier about certain things. But I'm also—
talking about superstition, something goes up,
it has to go down—I'm also being careful about
what I do. Where or when I would get down, I'm
not sure. I'm superstitious in that sense. Francis
is a liver, he's more expansive, so I can see him
saying that about someone like me. I like that."[38]

4

Travis Bickle

Taxi Driver (1976)
Martin Scorsese

"I believe that someone should become a person like other people."
—Travis Bickle

The first thing to understand about Travis Bickle is that he is not a "realistic" character. As vivid as Robert De Niro's performance makes him, his creation is not located in the tradition of realism from which, say, Marlon Brando's Terry Malloy in Kazan's *On the Waterfront* (1954) emerged. In *Taxi Driver*, when Cybill Shepherd's Betsy, trying to describe to Travis how she sees him, quotes Kris Kristofferson's song "The Pilgrim, Chapter 33" about a person who's "partly truth, partly fiction, a walking contradiction," she is being more true than her character is meant to know. Because Travis, who cold-bloodedly kills several people before the movie is over, is not just a dangerous psychopath. He actually makes no sense, and you don't need to be a clinician to see that.

The Trinity

The tortured but oddly charismatic character is, in fact, an incoherent text contrived by three solitary, sometimes angry, sometimes unhappy men: the film's star, Robert De Niro; its scriptwriter, Paul Schrader; and its director, Martin Scorsese.

Schrader was a film critic who had made some headway as a screenwriter but hit several personal snags as a promising project was falling apart. "I got hit with two other blows to the body at the same time," he told interviewer Richard Thompson in 1976. "[M]y marriage fell through, and the affair that caused the marriage to fall through fell through, all within the same four or five months. […] I got to wandering around at night; I couldn't sleep because I was so depressed. I'd stay in bed till four or five P.M. then I'd say, 'Well, I can get a drink now.' I'd get up and get a drink and take the bottle with me and start wandering around the streets in my car at night. After the bars closed, I'd go to pornography. I'd do this all night, till morning, and I did it for about three or four weeks, a very destructive syndrome, until I was saved from it by an ulcer; I had not been eating, just drinking. That was when the metaphor hit me for *Taxi Driver*, and I realized that this was the metaphor I had been looking for: the man who will take anybody any place for money; the man who moves through the city like a rat through the sewer; the man who is constantly surrounded by people, yet has no friends. The absolute symbol of urban loneliness. That's the thing I'd been living; that was my symbol, my metaphor. […] I wrote the script very quickly, in something like fifteen days. The script just jumped from my mind almost intact."[39]

The story that the intellectual Schrader (who authored the book *Transcendental Style in Film: Ozu, Bresson, Dreyer* before the fall he describes above) gave to Bickle may have its affinities with the likes of John Ford's *The Searchers* (1956), but Schrader is far less detached from Travis than John Ford was from Ethan Edwards. It's the directness of the connection between Schrader and Bickle that helps make the character compelling, but also imbues him with bizarre contradictions.

Scorsese seemed to have a slightly more conscious conception of Bickle and how he would fit into the movie. "Much of *Taxi Driver* arose from my feeling that movies really are a kind of dream-state, or like taking dope. And the shock of walking out of the theater into broad daylight can be terrifying. I watch movies all the time and I am also very bad at waking up. The film was like that for me—that sense of being almost awake."[40] For all the sense of trying to convey a particular mode of seeing, Scorsese also admitted, "I know this guy, Travis. I've had feelings he has and those feelings have to be explored, taken out, and examined."[41]

Stepping into Travis

If De Niro felt any overt identification with Travis Bickle beyond certain particulars of isolation and rejection (as any actor, including De Niro, will likely tell you, rejection is the salient feature of pretty much every performer's career), the taciturn actor has not talked about it. "There are underground things about yourself that you don't want to discuss. Somehow these things are better expressed on paper or on film."[42]

He threw himself into the role with customary vigor. Though Schrader had conceived Travis as a Midwestern guy transplanted to the big city, De Niro did not, as he had trekked to Georgia in preparation for his role in *Bang the Drum*

De Niro as Travis Bickle in a scene from the end of the film.

Slowly, travel to the heartland to research Travis. Instead, among other things, he embroiled himself in pathology. With Schrader, he read aloud into a tape recorder from the diaries of Arthur Bremer, the failed would-be assassin of politician George Wallace. Schrader had written the *Taxi Driver* script before the diaries had seen publication in 1973, but since that time Schrader had discovered that Bremer's fame-obsessed writings showed a distinctive affinity with Bickle's strivings to "become a person like other people"; those strivings end up also including a failed assassination attempt of a political figure.

De Niro also got a hack license and worked as a New York City cabbie for a period. Scorsese tells a story wherein De Niro is driving a cab shortly after his *Godfather Part II* Oscar win, and a fare recognizes him and is incredulous and concludes that things really *are* tough all over.

How Should a Person Be?

Taxi Driver introduces Travis Bickle outside of the film's diegesis. The movie opens with a particularly insistent horns-and-snare-drum cue from Bernard Herrmann's score and a smeary shot of steam gushing out of a manhole, through which a taxi emerges, like a ghost ship. The following shots have the abstract feel of an avant-garde short, but they're recognizably views of Manhattan's Times Square in what was, at the time of the film's making, the present day. (The Manhattan depicted in *Taxi Driver* has all but disappeared, which makes watching the film today a peculiar experience in ways audiences of the time may not have anticipated; sometimes it's like a science-fiction film.) Interspersed with these views, at least one of which is clearly from behind the driver's seat of a moving car, are shots of De Niro's eyes in medium close-up, as red and white and purple lights pass over his face. The eyes move back and forth, slowly, blankly. Then the steam again, and a view of Travis walking through a door … to apply for a job as a cab driver.

The supervisor, played with vintage New Yawk slob verisimilitude by Joe Spinell, is unusually solicitous of Bickle's innermost thoughts, and Bickle responds in a bluff manner that eventually earns the response "Are you gonna break my chops?" There's a distinct echo of *Mean Streets*' Johnny Boy as Travis grins, then smirks, after faking an apology. It's the only time in the movie that Travis is quite this glibly assured, and he doesn't grin like that again until after the cops enter the apartment where he sits, all bloodied up, after massacring the men who have been exploiting the teen prostitute Iris. Only then the grin is definitively tinged with madness. But after the little misunderstanding, Travis withdraws, and Spinnell becomes sympathetic again, and when Travis tells him he was in the Marines, he reaches out even more, and Travis responds with incomprehension to the question of whether he's "moonlighting." "What's moonlighting?" he says, brow furrowed in sad befuddlement.

After assuring Spinell's character that he'll work "anytime" and drive "anywhere," he gets the gig and hustles out of the garage. Then, an extraordinary visual: Travis coming out of the garage, walking up Fifty-seventh Street toward the camera in long shot, which dissolves to the same shot, just a few seconds later, of Travis farther up the street, still walking, chugging from a pint bottle of booze. "I borrowed the dissolve effect from George Stevens's film *Shane*," Scorsese says on an audio commentary for a home video version of *Taxi Driver*. "It's a scene where Jack Palance walks into the bar. The camera's at a very low angle, and he approaches the camera, and it dissolves to a much tighter shot of his boots as they approach the rain. I always found that fascinating." Indeed. One of the things that make it fascinating in the context of *Shane* (1953) is that there's no rational reason for it to be there, that as a stylistic touch it seems out of place with the ostensible classicism that cinephiles tend to associate with directors such as Stevens. But the flourish serves a function: it catches the viewer off guard, and gives a sense of Palance's villain being something like a supernatural agent. The dissolve serves a similar function in *Taxi Driver*, but rather than necessarily pegging Bickle as some kind of supernatural agent, the feeling is more, for lack of a better word, existential than metaphysical. Then there's the matter of his behavior: dissolving to a shot of Travis drinking on the street gives, even only minutes into the film, a sense of his being locked in to a destructive mode, on a loop that will have to be violently jumped if anything is ever going to change for him.

An Alienated Movie About Alienation

"All the animals come out at night," Travis is heard musing, in voice-over, as Scorsese and director of photography Michael Chapman's camera looks out of the passenger-side window of a cab at the prostitutes in short skirts and hot pants walking the street. Bickle's monologues almost dominate the film in this front section; they're meant to be passages from his diary, and De Niro recites them a grim flatness that's appropriate to their "prose": "Sick. Venal. Someday a real rain'll come and wash all the scum off the streets." Corresponding shots of Travis driving the cab, looking at the depraved panorama that the camera seems to capture in documentary style but is in fact largely the product of his own perception, show him slack-jawed. As he concocts his solution, Bickle will close his mouth, toughen up, and get into mission mode. But for now, he is wide-eyed.

Bickle persuades a taxi company "personnel officer" (played by Joe Spinell) to give him a job.

In a 2010 interview with *Esquire* magazine,[d] Jodie Foster gave the following account of her experience working with De Niro on *Taxi Driver* and how what she thought was her polished professionalism, honed over many years as a child actor and model, brought her up short.

"By the time I got the role in *Taxi Driver*, I'd already made more stuff than De Niro or Martin Scorsese. I'd been working from the time I was three years old. So even though I was only twelve, I felt like I was the veteran there. De Niro took me aside before we started filming. He kept picking me up from my hotel and taking me to different diners. The first time he basically didn't say anything. He would just, like, mumble. The second time he started to run lines with me, which was pretty boring because I already knew the lines. The third time, he ran lines with me again and now I was really bored. The fourth time, he ran lines with me, but then he started going off on these completely different ideas within the scene, talking about crazy things and asking me to follow in terms of improvisation.

"So we'd start with the original script and then he'd go off on some tangent and I'd have to follow, and then it was my job to eventually find the space to bring him back to the last three lines of the text we'd already learned.

"It was a huge revelation for me, because until that moment I thought being an actor was just acting naturally and saying the lines someone else wrote. Nobody had ever asked me to build a character. The only thing they'd ever done to direct me was to say something like 'Say it faster' or 'Say it slower.' So it was a whole new feeling for me, because I realized acting was not a dumb job. You know, I thought it was a dumb job. Somebody else writes something and then you repeat it. Like, how dumb is that?

"There was this moment, in some diner somewhere, when I realized for the first time that it was me who hadn't brought enough to the table. And I felt this excitement where you're all sweaty and you can't eat and you can't sleep."

This makes no sense when you extrapolate from the perspective of normal plausibility. When Bickle applies for the hack job, he tells the personnel guy that he wants to drive a cab because he can't sleep. "There's porno theaters for that," the personnel guy shoots back. Travis tells him he's tried that. The character is clearly in the know about the seamy side of the city. (Indeed, *Taxi Driver*'s city is entirely seamy, in contrast to the more genteel Manhattan depicted in Woody Allen's *Annie Hall* (1977), shot on location only about a year after *Taxi Driver* was filmed.) His inability to make a connection—his fumbling with the concession stand girl at the porno theater (played by De Niro's then-girlfriend, Diahnne Abbott, whom he would marry in 1976) is poignant, while his insistence after his initial rejection is troubling—is almost always awkward in the most extreme way possible. But the movie is always *with* him; its depiction of the film's normal, productive members of society—Cybill Shepherd's Betsy and her coworker Tom (Albert Brooks), campaigners for a presidential candidate—clearly takes place from an uncomfortable remove.

If *Taxi Driver* is a movie about alienation (an admittedly fuzzy and too-often catchall term), it's an alienated movie about alienation. While Schrader and Scorsese may seem, at some points, to be manipulating Bickle to flaunt their own perceived status as outsiders, De Niro functions as a rational player in the dynamic by doing their bidding with unwavering commitment, regardless of the discrete task he's asked to perform and whether or not it truly fits into a "coherent" pattern.

The hosannas of many of its admirers notwithstanding, *Taxi Driver* is not a gritty, bloody urban drama with an ambivalent/ironic view of vigilante justice. It is an irrational film. And as such, De Niro's performance is both remarkable and unusually deliberate in its willingness to go out on every limb it requires.

Looking at De Niro/Bickle

Some of the movie's most extraordinary moments emerge from the way Scorsese looks at Bickle/De Niro, and the way he *doesn't* look at De Niro/Bickle. Take the scene in which Bickle tries to "hang out" with his fellow cabbies in a diner; the way he half raises his eyebrows perfunctorily in response to a salacious anecdote, his glare at the question "How's it hanging?" the intensity of his gaze as he looks at the black pimps at another table, sitting more or less immobile in front of their burgers and cans of Schaefer. Travis puts a couple of Alka-Seltzer tablets into a glass of water and the soundtrack is filled with their fizz, and Scorsese cuts to a low-angle shot of Travis's face as he looks into the glass, and De Niro's expression, his mouth slightly open, is poised perfectly between

the beatific and the catatonic. The camera moves up, tightening in on his face, and he's utterly immobile and his pupils look back. Scorsese then cuts to a matching moving-camera shot from Travis's point of view, into the fizzing bubbling glass and its white nothingness. Again, this is a cinematic homage, to the close-up of brown bubbles in a cup of coffee in Jean-Luc Godard's 1967 film *2 ou 3 choses que je sais d'elle* (*2 or 3 Things I Know About Her*), but the difference is what's being depicted, and in this equation Godard comes out looking like the optimist; the coffee bubbles evoke a teeming cosmos, while the dull white bicarbonate bubbles in the water speak of an unending blankness, a void.

Similarly, there's the infamous shot of Travis speaking to Betsy on a pay phone after he has, disastrously, taken her to a porno theater on their first and only date. De Niro acts with a defeated stillness as he tries to make small talk, and he absorbs each of her denials (which are not heard on the soundtrack) stoically. And it seems the camera just can't stand to watch: it tracks to the right and settles on a view down a hallway, past some elevators, of the building's front door. "That was the first shot I thought of in the film, and it was the last I filmed," Scorsese says. "I liked it because I sensed that it added to the loneliness of the whole thing, but I guess you can see the hand behind the camera there."[43] Yes, you can. But that's not a bad thing.

Mission Mode

Travis Bickle's various and sundry attempts to realize his belief that "someone should become a person like other people" lead him to act in ways that seem very real-world improbable, even taking into account how disturbed he is. Bickle's time with the Marines, in Vietnam, is alluded to at the beginning but never spoken of again. It's very directly evoked when, prior to the film's climax, he gives himself a mohawk haircut. But because the Vietnam theme was introduced and abandoned almost instantaneously, the haircut comes as a shock, and that's whether or not the viewer understands what it refers to. Scorsese: "A friend of mine named Victor Magnotta [...] was going to be a priest, but when Vietnam broke out he went into the Special Forces. [...] He told us that, in Saigon, if you saw a guy with his head shaved—like a little Mohawk—that usually meant those people were ready to go into a certain Special Forces situation. You didn't even go near them. They were ready to kill. They were in a psychological and emotional mode to go. He showed us a picture: the Mohawk was shorter than the one in the film, but pretty close. And Bob had the idea. This is a story where Bob says 'I had the idea' and I go 'No, I had the idea.' I'll give it to him."[44]

While the idea came from a real-life situation, from a form of research, thrown up on screen it seems to leap out from a nightmare. As does the

weird reversal of Travis' date with Betsy. He does everything pretty much right. He dresses nicely, buys a modest gift, all that. And then brings her into a porno theater. The contradictions were major irritants to the critics Manny Farber and Patricia Patterson, who in their essay "The Power and the Gory" wrote, "Though De Niro rarely changes speed inside a scene, from scene to scene his Bickle figure is a whirligig with his IQ and sophistication shifting and sliding all over the place."[45]

But throughout it all De Niro is entirely stalwart. (Asked in a 1981 symposium if Travis Bickle made sense to him, De Niro responded, "You know, everybody always says you have to explain certain things [...]. I make it work for myself."[46]) "Were Mr. De Niro less of an actor, the character would be a sideshow freak,"[47] *New York Times* critic Vincent Canby observed.It is a possibly instructive, in this context, to cite De Niro's exchange with Lawrence Grobel about the character. "I got this image of Travis as a crab," De Niro said. "You know how a crab sort of walks sideways and has a gawky, awkward movement?" Grobel countered, "Not straightforward?" and De Niro clarified, "No, not devious in that sense. Crabs are very straightforward, but straightforward to them is going to the left and to the right. They turn sideways; that's the way they're built."[48]

Rock Stars

On their trip to a diner near the campaign headquarters where Travis first asks Betsy out, Betsy tells him that she's never met anyone like him before, and that he reminds her of the lyrics to a song. She recites them: "He's a poet/he's a pusher," and Travis immediately takes strong exception, protesting that he's never pushed drugs. (Bickle's inability to take anything not literally is a *relatively* consistent hallmark of his character.) She then insists that the crux of what she's getting at has to do with the lines "partly truth, partly fiction, a walking contradiction." If you haven't heard the song "The Pilgrim, Chapter 33" by Kris Kristofferson, from his 1971 album *The Silver Tongued Devil and I,* you might assume this "Pilgrim" is some sort of allegorical figure. In the song's spoken-word prologue, which Kristofferson speaks in a boozy drawl that makes part of his spiel tough to understand, he says it's about his fellow artistes, some specific ones at that. "I started writin' this song about Chris Gantry ..." Chris Gantry was/is a Nashville Music Row songwriter whose most famous tune was/is Glen Campbell's "Dreams of an Everyday Housewife." Kristofferson continues: "... end up writin' about Dennis Hopper, Johnny Cash, Norman ... Norbert ... Funky Donnie Fred ... [incomprehensible] Swan, Bobby Neuwirth ..."

Then there's the matter of Bickle's mirror monologue, the famed "You talkin' to me?"

bit. Credited by all involved to De Niro, in early anecdotes and commentaries Scorsese remembers that De Niro lifted/adapted the phrase and its attendant self-answers ("'Cause I'm the only one here") from a stand-up comic he had seen around the time of the shoot. In his 2009 anecdotal autobiography *Big Man: Real Life & Tall Tales,* Clarence Clemons, the saxophonist for Bruce Springsteen's E Street Band, recalls hanging out with De Niro and the actor making a "confession." After swearing Clemons to silence for twenty-five years, De Niro asks Clemons if he remembers "the thing I do" in *Taxi Driver,* and of course Clemons does, and De Niro tells him, "It's not original. I stole the whole thing." From Clemons's boss, referred to by radio DJs across the United States as "The Boss," in fact. Clemons has De Niro saying, "He did it in concert. At some point he's got the whole fucking crowd in a frenzy. Everybody's on their feet screaming their lungs out and saying his name, and he stops in the spotlight and looks out into this howling mass of people, and as cool as a fucking cucumber he says 'Are you talking to me? To me? Is that who you're talking to? Are you talking to me?' Fucking brilliant."[49]

Locating Bickle's undeniable negativity-infused magnetism in the vicinity of rock star charisma may not have been inapt, but it can't be said to have helped certain people understand the movie properly, as the world and Scorsese and De Niro and Jodie Foster and Ronald Reagan learned a few years later. De Niro's reprise of "You talkin' to me?" in a very bad children's movie two decades after Foster-obsessed John Hinckley tried to assassinate then-president Reagan played as sacrilege to many. For De Niro, it may have just been a way of distancing, defusing, walking away from an uncomfortable truth he hadn't even known he had articulated at the time.

The now famous line Bickle delivers to his image in the mirror: "You talkin' to me?"

Following pages: Bang, bang: Bickle facing police officers after his killing spree.

5

Jake La Motta

Raging Bull (1980)
Martin Scorsese

"I got no choice! I got no choice!"
—Jake La Motta

Martin Scorsese tells the disturbing story of how *Raging Bull* came to be: "*New York, New York* was a flop; my second marriage had broken up; my second child was born, I started living with Robbie Robertson, and went through so many drugs that I almost destroyed myself completely. [...] My body gave way. I was 109 pounds (I'm 155 pounds now) and I couldn't get myself back together physically and psychologically. [...] Basically, I was dying; I was bleeding internally all over and I didn't know it. My eyes were bleeding, my hands, everything except my brain and my liver. I was coughing up blood. [...] [N]ext thing I knew I was in the emergency ward at the New York Hospital. The doctors took care of me for ten days. And Bob came to visit me."[50]

"We can make this picture," De Niro reportedly said, berating his friend, a man with whom he had formed a brotherly bond over the last portion of a decade. "We can really do a great job. Are we doing it or not?"[51]

De Niro's Choice

If Scorsese was at a life and a career nadir, De Niro himself was riding high. Since making *Taxi Driver*, De Niro had worked on *The Last Tycoon* with Kazan. The result was not an artistic success, but the film was a big-scale production featuring an all-star cast. And the association with Kazan placed him squarely in the iconic firmament with Brando. His international profile was upped by his appearance in Bernardo Bertolucci's gonzo Marxist epic *1900* (1976), opposite Gerard Depardieu. He led an ensemble cast of acting contemporaries (including Christopher Walken, John Cazale, and Meryl Streep) in Michael Cimino's *The Deer Hunter* (1978), still one of the most celebrated films of what has come to be known as the "Easy Riders, Raging Bulls" era of Hollywood filmmaking. Scorsese's complex, grueling *New York, New York* (1977), which still plays today like an uneasy but fascinating mix of Cassavetes and Minnelli (Vincente, the director, not Liza, his and Judy Garland's daughter and De Niro's costar in the film), flopped, but nobody blamed that on the actor.

Raging Bull was made at the behest of De Niro. The actor had been interested in the project for some time. He and Scorsese and Schrader had all come upon the book of the same title, a quasi-autobiography of the middleweight boxer Jake La Motta, around 1974, and one of the book's coauthors, sportswriter Peter Savage, has a bit part in *Taxi Driver*. La Motta, whose nickname was "the Bronx Bull," was a middleweight boxer who was a special favorite among white working-class New Yorkers. He was a most tenacious and ferocious rival to Sugar Ray Robinson, and his climb to the middleweight championship in 1950 was an arduous one that included one infamously fixed fight. In a post-championship fight, he took a beating from Robinson that entered boxing legend, not least due to the fact that La Motta, although he lost by a TKO, never went down. After La Motta's retirement from boxing, he ran bars and nightclubs, which brought him some trouble in 1958, when he was charged in Miami with introducing patrons to underage girls in his nightclub there. He protested his innocence but wound up on a chain gang anyway. After his release, he dabbled in film acting and as a nightclub entertainer.

One of the writers who took a crack at *Raging Bull* (after Scorsese's *Mean Streets* collaborator Mardik Martin) was Paul Schrader, with whom De Niro and Scorsese had worked on *Taxi Driver*. There was no way these three were going to collaborate on a "normal" boxing movie, not even of the sort with working-class origins such as *Somebody Up There Likes Me* (1956), the Rocky Graziano biopic starring Newman. And indeed the focal point of Schrader's treatment was La Motta's sexual obsessiveness. (His eleven-year marriage to Vickie La Motta, whom La Motta wed when she was sixteen, was an explosive one, marked by jealous rages and physical fights.) When Scorsese was well, he and De Niro decamped to the Caribbean island of Saint Martin and spent a couple of weeks rewriting the Schrader version of the script, coming to a mutual understanding of who they believed La Motta as a character was and how they were like him.

De Niro was remarkably forthcoming to Mary Pat Kelly, a writer and filmmaker who had corresponded with Scorsese since 1966, about the crafting of the *Raging Bull* script, and the fact

Robert De Niro in fighting pose as boxing champion Jack La Motta, aka "the Bronx Bull."

De Niro as Jack La Motta taking tips on style from the former middleweight champion himself.

Opposite top: The first match sequence in the film: the fight between La Motta and Jimmy Reeves (Floyd Anderson).

Opposite bottom: La Motta in a post-match row with his then-wife, played by Lori Anne Flax.

that while he and Scorsese did not subscribe to La Motta's overall philosophy of life, such as it was, they certainly understood where it was coming from: "Marty and I talked about how people had this kind of hippie attitude towards relationships. Everybody is so accepting. At the time. People were saying 'I don't care what she does,' or 'I don't care what he does,' and, 'If you really love the person, you won't make demands,' but to me and Marty, that attitude was a lot of bullshit. It was ignoring basic emotions. It was saying you have no right to feel them, and if you do you're a jerk and you're not hip. It's a lot of bullshit! The fact is, you're entitled to have those feelings. Some people may really feel they don't have them, but they're unusual."[52]

Defeats His Own Purpose

With the exception of *New York, New York*'s Jimmy Doyle, whose initial ebullience masks the bullheadedness his character shows in subsequent scenes, all of the characters in De Niro's first films with Scorsese come out of the gate as deeply damaged, problematic people. Johnny Boy in *Mean Streets* is first seen committing a not-innocuous act of vandalism. *Taxi Driver*'s Travis Bickle doesn't *develop* into a basket case; he *is* a basket case, albeit a pretty phantasmagorical one.

Raging Bull introduces Jake La Motta three times. First the credits sequence, one of the great tone-setters in cinema. To the strains of a tune from the opera *Cavalleria Rusticana*, a slow-motion shot of De Niro's La Motta in the boxing ring, three ropes framing and bisecting him as he bounces in his robe, swinging at the foggy air; the credit announcing the movie's title is in deep red, contrasting the black-and-white of the image and announcing that black-and-white as an artistic choice. Then the one-two punch of De Niro's La Motta in 1964 overweight nightclub entertainer mode, contrasted with his boxing trim of 1941.

The 1941 fight with the African-American boxer Jimmy Reeves ferociously telegraphs the repellent attitudes prevalent in La Motta's milieu. In between rounds, La Motta's brother, Joey, berates the fighter, asking, "Why the fuck do we have to come to Cleveland for you to get beaten by a moulignon?" "Moulignon" is Italian dialect for "eggplant" and was a racial epithet used by Italian-Americans. The "outpointed" La Motta responds petulantly: "You wanna go in there?" Then he gets into the ring and knocks Reeves down. Three times. He loses the fight anyway. Back home in the Bronx he gives his (first) wife and his downstairs neighbor a staggering, but it appears not-atypical, hard time. (Kicking up a fuss over an ostensibly overcooked steak, he complains, "It defeats its own purpose," before overturning the kitchen table; he then threatens to eat his neighbor's yapping dog, and at being called an "animal" he responds ,"Who's an animal? Your *mother's* an animal, you son of a bitch.")

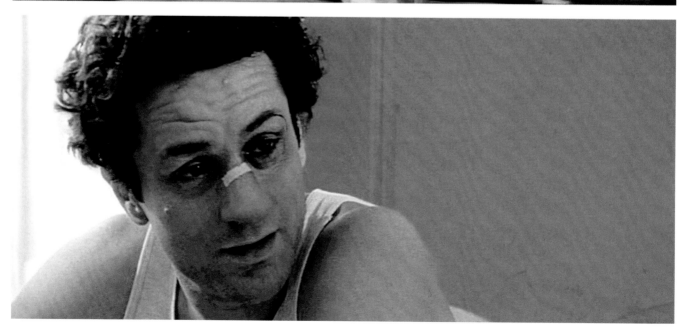

Opposite: La Motta complains
to his brother and manager,
Joey (Joe Pesci), "I ain't never
gonna get a chance to fight
the best there is."

La Motta waits for Vickie, to
whom Joey has finally agreed
to introduce him.

Following pages: La Motta and
his new love, soon-to-be-
second-wife, Vickie (Cathy
Moriarty).

When brother Joey turns up to commiserate over the loss, Jake indulges in some atypical introspection. "I got these small hands, I got these little girl's hands," he says to Joey, turning them over on the table.

Joey: "I got 'em too, what's the difference?"

"You know what that means? No matter how big I get, no matter who I fight, no matter what I do, I ain't never gonna fight Joe Lewis."

"Yeah, that's right. He's a heavyweight, you're a middleweight. We know that."

"I ain't never gonna get a chance to fight the best there is. And you know something? I'm better than him. I ain't never gonna get a chance." De Niro sits still, but still in a different way than the slowed-down La Motta of 1964. He turns to Joey. "And you're asking me what's wrong …"

Unattainable Absolutes

Less than fifteen minutes into the film, we are at the heart of the matter: La Motta's self-defeating obsession with unattainable absolutes. As it becomes clear that even the middleweight title is impossible unless La Motta plays ball with local mob interests (which he initially refuses to do, the viewer is led to surmise, not out of a surfeit of integrity, but just because), La Motta woos and wins the gorgeous teenage Vickie (Cathy Moriarty, who, like Pesci and supporting player Frank Vincent, was a relative novice to film and

untrained). But it's not enough that he marries her. Even as he masochistically denies himself her beauty (the pre-bout clinch with her he breaks free of, protesting he can't "mess around" before a fight, after which he pours ice water down his boxer shorts, is one of the most jaw-dropping in a film replete with jaw-dropping moments), he's compelled to possess her utterly, and when he can't, he throws rash accusations at her and at the people he's closest to, including his own brother. "When's it enough?" his brother asks Jake at one point, and the answer seems to be never.

One of Scorsese's short films from the 1960s was *The Big Shave* (1967), a simple account of a man who, on beginning to shave in a very white bathroom, cuts open his face and continues on, oblivious to the fact that with every stroke he's drawing more blood. Eventually his face, and the bathroom, are a crimson mess. Scorsese's men can't stop hurting themselves, and La Motta is an extreme example of that. ("Jake La Motta [Robert De Niro] defeats his own purpose," read a droll mid-eighties summary for a rep showing of the movie at New York's Cinema Village.)

Often the movie explicitly takes La Motta's perspective, particularly his early views of Vickie. Scorsese includes luxuriant, slow-motion shots of Moriarty's feet and calves in the water of the public swimming pool where La Motta first meets her, not unlike the slo-mo view of Cybill Sheperd's Betsy in *Taxi Driver*. The boxing sequences, often

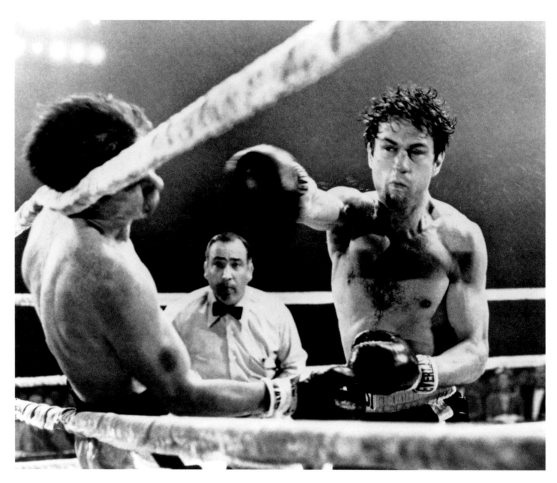

cited for their incredible realism and brutality, are filled with quickly-cut shots of De Niro's character taking incredible punishment, and sometimes meting it out. In contrast to most of the movies featuring boxing sequences up until that time, the camera is almost always inside the ring. "De Niro came up with a brilliant idea. He had a punching bag put in the ring. He'd be up there punching and when he'd jump to the spot where we were shooting, he was already worked up," Scorsese recounted.[53]

The actor also studied boxing, sometimes with La Motta himself, who gave him tips on style; De Niro soaked these up while picking up clues to La Motta's personality. Interestingly though, De Niro does not genuinely mimic La Motta's boxing style in the fight scenes, instead emphasizing certain aspects for the camera. His crouch is a little more severe than La Motta's; he charges out to the ring in more of a hurry than the actual boxer did. Not to underplay the very real violence of La Motta's style, but looking at old films of his bouts one gets the impression of a somewhat more thoughtful pugilist than the one De Niro brings to life in Scorsese's film.

Dreams and Improvisations

The domestic scenes are unstinting in their persistence, their determination to stay in a very uncomfortable place as Jake deliberately escalates the tension. For instance, in the scene where Vickie casually observes that an upcoming ring opponent is "good-looking" and Jake gives her the third degree over it. (He subsequently, sadistically, almost mutilates that opponent in the fight, leaving a mobster in the audience to muse, "He ain't pretty no more.") Or, perhaps even worse, when Jake confronts Joey with the impossible question "You fuck my wife?" Martin Scorsese notes, "Bob is a very generous actor and he will be even stronger when the other guy's in close-up. Often I steal lines from the speeches we film over his shoulder, because some of them are so good. And he really gets other actors to act in his scenes. For example, when Jake asks Joey, 'Did you fuck my wife?' I had written a seven-page scene, the only full-length dialogue scene in the film. When he asks the question, you see Joey asking him back, 'What, how could you say that?' I told Bob I wasn't getting enough reaction from Joe Pesci. He told me to roll the camera again, and then said, 'Did you fuck your mother?' When you see the film again, look at Joe's reaction! I like that kind of help. You have to throw your ego out of the door: you can't take it into the rehearsal room and you can't take it on the set."[54]

The steady compositions of the shots, the almost dreamy quality of the black-and-white photography (as with *Taxi Driver*, the cinematographer here is Michael Chapman), and the way the film goes from scene to scene without placing particular emphasis on the life events

that would be big moments in a conventional sports-themed biographical film give the movie the quality of a dream—a frequently very bad dream—rather than a fact-based, realist chronicle. For instance, the title fight La Motta so long coveted, against Marcel Cerdan, is given arguably less stress than La Motta's pre-fight freakout after seeing the mob boss who got him the match kissing Vickie in greeting. The fleeting gesture at that fight's conclusion of La Motta going to Cerdan's corner and embracing him as the decision is announced is strangely moving in precisely such a dreamlike way; it's almost like something out of Cocteau.

When the film finally settles in with La Motta in his 1964 mode, he is portrayed, despite his portly stature and heavy breathing, as a man who's somehow found some peace with himself. The movie concludes with a passage from the New Testament and a dedication to Haig Manoogian, an NYU professor and mentor of Scorsese's, who died in the spring of 1980.

But the movie never shows La Motta achieving an epiphany, finding a state of grace. We are left with his resigned composure in the dressing room of the Barbizon Plaza, which is depicted about ten minutes after his wailing meltdown in the Dade County Stockade in 1957. There, in those shadows, De Niro/La Motta painfully punches the walls (in maybe the one concession to common sense made in De Niro's relentless pursuit of

authenticity for the role, the wall he hits with his bare fists was a rubberized one), calls himself stupid, and moans that he's "not an animal."

Was this an exorcism? The film does not tell us; it merely breaks off the line and begins another in a quieter register. A friend and fellow critic, in conversation about the movie, said to me admiringly, "It's not even really a 'film,' it's more like a poem." But De Niro's performance is a protean film performance. While his La Motta is a more "consistent" character than Travis Bickle, the portrayal required equal conscientiousness to achieve. In a sense De Niro embodies a reality principle that grounds both the character and the movie. And here lies a key to the De Niro myth, because as good a performance as he may give in any other film, the practically numinous quality arises only out of the particular concatenations of talents and themes that *Taxi Driver* and *Raging Bull* provided.

"Give Me a Stage/Where This Bull Here Can Rage"

At the time of its release, *Raging Bull* was met with frustration and incomprehension by some reviewers and no doubt many audience members (the complaint continues on movie sites on the Internet to this day) that, despite being excellently portrayed, almost all of its characters, particularly Jake, were not "likable," or, worse, "relatable." The most eloquent of the

protesters in this vein was the critic Pauline Kael, who wrote, "Listening to Jake and Joey go at each other, like the macho clowns in Cassavetes movies, I know I'm supposed to be responding to powerful, ironic realism, but I just feel trapped. Jake says 'You dumb f—k,' and Joey says 'You dumb f—k,' and they repeat it and repeat it. And I think, What am I doing here watching these two dumb f—ks?"[55] The passage, of course, has an unmistakable whiff of lamentable classist condescension, but one can't argue with the proposition that if you are unable to key into the characters and their concerns, the movie is not going to do much for you. Andrew Sarris, in his *Village Voice* review of the film, stated, "What has always puzzled me is why anyone would want to make a movie about Jake La Motta."[56]

Robin Wood, in his study *Hollywood from Vietnam to Reagan*, tries to work things through more thoroughly: "The meaning the film finally seems to offer its audience—La Motta's progress toward partial understanding, acceptance or 'grace'—must strike one as quite inadequate to validate the project, and actually misleading: the film remains extremely vague about the nature of the grace or how it has been achieved. Any suggestion of that kind is in fact thoroughly outweighed by the sense the film conveys of pointless and *unredeemed* pain, both the pain La Motta experiences and the pain he inflicts. But, if one rejects the film's invitation (at best half-hearted, and deriving, one may assume, more from Schrader than Scorsese) to read it in terms of a movement toward salvation, one must accept the invitation to read it centrally as a character study (though 'case history' might be the more felicitous term). The film's fragmented structure can be read as determined by La Motta's own incoherence, by Scorsese's fascination with that incoherence and with the violence that is its product."[57]

Wood goes on to examine the movie's homosexual subtext, a subtext that Scorsese has allowed is indeed there. Wood's reasoning, drawing from Freud, is both provocative and persuasive. For instance: "The film counterpoints two forms of violence: violence against women and violence against men, the latter subdivided between the socially licensed violence in the ring and the socially disapproved violence in public and private places outside the ring. While the motivations for these three different manifestations of violence may seem quite distinct—Jakes pursuit of a boxing career, his jealousy concerning Vickie—I think a true understanding of the film depends on our ability to grasp the relation between them."[58] But part of what makes the film such a rich and richly disquieting experience is the intuitive grasp of that relation, and of other relations that the various components of the picture working in tandem make possible.

And despite all of the awful acts that *Raging Bull* depicts Jake La Motta perpetrating, the actor who portrayed him had some personal, perhaps intuitive, investment in "doing right" by his difficult character. "What we wanted with Jake was to have something that was very straightforward," De Niro told Mary Pat Kelly. "Jake himself is primitive, he can't hide certain feelings. I worked with Jake, the real Jake La Motta. I would pick his brain. There are a lot of things going on in there. I admired the fact that he was at least willing to question himself and his actions. But what's he going to do? Should he be like a college professor and try to say 'Well, I think the reason that I did that was because …' He would talk that way sometimes, but he was more cunning. He'd look at you dead-pan, or he'd laugh about certain things. He would protect himself sometimes, but then he would say, 'Aah, I was a son-of-a-bitch.' I always thought that there was something very decent about him somewhere."[59]

Opposite: scenes depicting La Motta's life in the 1960s:

Top left: Charged with having introduced underage girls to clients at his club, he removes stones from his championship belt to help pay his defense.

Top right: La Motta in his new role as nightclub owner and stand-up entertainer.

Bottom: The scene at Jake La Motta's eponymous club just before Vickie announces that she is finally leaving him.

6

Rupert Pupkin

The King of Comedy (1983)
Martin Scorsese

"*Mom!*"
—Rupert Pupkin

The controversy/misunderstanding with respect to *Raging Bull*'s ultimate value as a narrative motion picture notwithstanding, the movie would go on to win two Oscars: Best Actor for De Niro, and Best Film Editing, awarded to Thelma Schoonmaker. (When future husband Michael Powell congratulated her on the award, she responded furiously: "I didn't deserve it, and you know I didn't deserve it. Marty should have gotten the Oscar, not me."[60]) The Oscar ceremony that had been scheduled to take place on Monday, March 30, 1981, was postponed for an evening because of a failed assassination attempt on President Ronald Reagan. It subsequently emerged that the would-be assassin, John Warnock Hinckley Jr., was obsessed with, and had been stalking, the actress Jodie Foster; that he had seen the film *Taxi Driver* more than a dozen times; and that he had concocted his presidential assassination scheme as a way to impress Foster. As he was arrested, Hinckley reportedly asked the law officers taking him into custody whether they thought his actions would cause a postponement of the Oscars ceremony.

On winning the Best Actor Oscar, De Niro, ever ill-at-ease in the spotlight, ended his acceptance speech by thanking "everyone […] involved in the film, and I hope that I can share this with anyone that it means anything to and the rest of world and especially with all the terrible things that are happening."[61] Backstage in the press room, responding to questions about the possible connection between Hinckley's assassination attempt and *Taxi Driver*, the actor squirmed: "I don't know about the story; I don't want to discuss the matter now." When pressed, he continued, "I said what I wanted to say out there. You're all very nice, but that's it."[62]

A Response to Celebrity-Worship Culture?

In several not at all unreasonable respects, *The King of Comedy* can be read as a response to the suddenly (or so it seemed) violent turn that celebrity culture, and celebrity-worship culture, took with the John Lennon murder in late 1980 and the Reagan assassination attempt mere

months later. But the script for *The King of Comedy* dated back to the early seventies. The writer, Paul D. Zimmerman (himself, like frequent Scorsese collaborator Jay Cocks, a film critic, for *Newsweek*) conceived the notion for the story after watching an episode of *The David Susskind Show* (a staple of New York talk television in the sixties) about autograph hunters and noting "the intimacy with which [they] spoke of these people they didn't really know … Like 'Barbra's really tough to work with.' Which means, Barbra Streisand told them to shove it up their ass."[63]

And as with *Raging Bull*, the impetus to make it was initially much stronger on De Niro's part than on Scorsese's. "Of all my films, *The King of Comedy* is the one that comes closest to a straight narrative. After *Alice* [*Doesn't Live Here Anymore*, the 1974 feature with which Scorsese followed *Mean Streets*], I wasn't ready for it. It seemed to me that it would be a film about just one gag: the kidnapping,"[64] Scorsese told Michael Henry Wilson in 1983. "After I took *Alice, Taxi Driver, New York, New York*, and *Raging Bull* around the world to different festivals, I took a look at the script again and I had a different take on it," Scorsese elaborated to Richard Schickel years later. "I began to understand what Bob's association with it was, what he went through after *Mean Streets*, certainly after *Godfather II*— the adulation of the crowd, and the strangers who love you and have got to be with you and have got to say things."[65]

Rupert Pupkin's New York

The King of Comedy begins, after a glimpse of *The Jerry Langford Show* (a nearly pitch-perfect pastiche of *The Tonight Show*; that program's then-host, Johnny Carson, had been approached to play the Langford role) with a scrum of autograph seekers outside the show's stage door. De Niro's Rupert Pupkin strides into the crowd with a combination of confidence and wariness. The autograph seekers, a motley bunch, recognize him as one of their own; "Hey, Rupert, who'd you get?" they ask, and he responds with annoyance. "Sidney, I'm really not that interested. It's not my whole life." The viewer can't know on first viewing that what ensues—Rupert "saving" talk show host Jerry Langford from a single

Rupert Pupkin: stand-up comedian or psychopath?

crazed fan, and then pitching himself as a comic to Jerry on the subsequent limo ride he more or less hijacks—was contrived in advance, that the "crazed fan" Rupert delivers Jerry from is Rupert's friend and co-conspirator Masha. It is extremely telling that, before anything even happens, Rupert is already high-hatting it over his kind, acting superior to them. There are many who consider the depiction of Rupert repellent, and watching *The King of Comedy* with foreknowledge of its events gives the viewer an even less favorable impression of the character than they might have had first time around.

It's hard to know what to make of the character, and of De Niro, in this opening scene. The movie is set in the time it was made, the early eighties, and as a person walking the streets of New York City, Pupkin looks more anachronistic than any character played by De Niro in a New York–set film, whether directed by Scorsese or not. Aside from his face, which is heavier, blockier, than it appears in the films of that time in which he's depicting a physical prime, his goofy, helmet-like hairdo and thick but well-trimmed moustache set him apart. The sport jacket he's wearing, light blue, could be wool or could be polyester; it's hard to tell. The shirt-and-tie combo is a beaut: the shirt is navy blue with a white collar, the tie red; it's very American flag. In longer shots we see that the kerchief in the pocket of his sport jacket matches the tie exactly. He looks like the mook's conception of a comedian or talk show host. And when he finally meets up with Langford, we see him in contrast with the real thing. Langford's jacket, gray-blue, is clearly of superior fabric, his shirt a tasteful light blue, his tie a muted red; there's no kerchief in the jacket pocket. Pupkin is thus possibly understood as a mutated doppelgänger of Langford, as a William Wilson figure who got messed up in the teleportation phase, perhaps.

Pupkin's partner in crime, Masha, is an odder than average duck as well. While we don't get a lot of backstory on her, she's clearly got means. Played by Sandra Bernhard, then a comedian/performance artist and a screen novice, she dresses like a third-hand idea of an Ivy League misfit. If Rupert's mode of presentation is aggression that thinks it's passive-aggression, Masha is overtly hostile in her sexual advances to Jerry once she gets her part of the deal—she holds him captive at her town house while Rupert goes off to the television appearance they kidnapped Jerry to engineer. Bernard's performance gets particular resonance out of her willingness to use a no-holds-barred gawky physicality in her seduction of Langford.

Two Kings

As De Niro's career continues, and he begins to fall into a series of roles in movies that seem to critics and admirers like work for the sake of just a paycheck or the work itself—what's regularly referred to in the reviewing world as hackwork—what remains consistent, if not necessarily as arresting as it used to be, is the quality of attention he brings to his one-on-one exchanges.

His back-and-forth with Jerry Lewis in *The King of Comedy* is particularly startling, for several reasons. First there's the division of the exchanges themselves. After the limo scene, there's not much contact between Pupkin and Jerry Langford until the disastrous "house party," and then the kidnapping, during which the relationship between the two characters, such as it is, turns hostile, Jerry's attempt at humanizing himself for his captors notwithstanding. But several scenes in the movie, which ramp up the delusions of grandeur that lead Rupert to believe that he can just hop on a train and go visit Jerry at his Long Island retreat, depict Rupert's dreams or visions of his relationship, a cozy but still competitive showbiz friendship in which the two men relate to each other as equals.

Only minutes after the real Langford, condescendingly but not without a grudging admiration for Pupkin's gall, says to his fan, "I think once you get over the initial shyness, you're going to be okay," and the joke flies right over Pupkin's blocky head, Rupert (after gazing down at the monogrammed handkerchief he's taken from Langford; even here he is scheming) has a reverie in which he and Langford are lunching at, of course, Sardi's, then still a potent signifier of New York showbiz life. Langford is grave; he has a favor to ask Pupkin. Jerry Lewis, whose performance here is one of the highlights in a career this Lewis fan will aver is full of such things (a lot of the sub–conventional wisdom pertaining to *The King of Comedy* is that it's one of the very few genuinely worthwhile things Lewis has put his name to, a notion appalling in its ignorance and presumption), plays the exchange absolutely straight. De Niro, on the other hand, is doing something else; as Pupkin inside of Pupkin's dream, he depicts Pupkin preparing to be the new showbiz god that Jerry Langford, of all people, has to ask a favor of. When Langford thanks Pupkin for meeting him for lunch ("I know how busy you are, I know how tired you are"), De Niro, his jaw slack, his cheeks puffier than normal, even for this role, breathes in, puffs up his cheeks some more, and thinks, as if wondering how not to give the game away. "What are friends for, Jerry?" he responds, and then relaxes a bit and proceeds to smarmily apply unctuous concern to his onetime idol, telling him how tired he looks. This leads Jerry back to a topic that is the subject of Rupert's fantasy: a request to guest-host Langford's show for a few weeks. Scorsese's camera comes out of its pattern of reversing close-ups to a medium shot of the table. Behind Pupkin and Langford, a caricaturist in Sardi's employ is sketching them. "Listen, I really wish you would

Top: De Niro as Rupert Pupkin, autograph hunter and would-be stand-up comedian.

Bottom: Pupkin and the "staged" rescue of his hero, Jerry Langford (Jerry Lewis) from a crazed fan.

Opposite: The first of Pupkin's imagined conversations with Langford, in which his hero begs his help with his show.

Jerry Lewis, director Martin Scorsese, and Robert De Niro on the set of the movie.

think about it again," Lewis's Langford pleads. Rupert begins gesticulating. It's not a conversation anymore, it's schtick. "How can I not think about it?" Rupert protests, now seen in the isolation of a room postered with images of Langford and other showbiz personalities. He's talking to himself. "I can't even take over my own life for six weeks," he wails, and from another room a woman calls out "Rupert ..." "What?" Rupert shouts back, trying not to break the spell. "What are you doing down there so late?" Rupert returns to his reverie, but is soon interrupted again: "Rupert, who are you talking to?" "Mom ... please stop calling me!" he calls back in annoyance.

Comedy Dues-Paying and Its Discontents

Successful performers, most frequently comedians, often tell anecdotes of humiliation and failure on the road to fame, and of the stupid/ naïve things they themselves did while learning "the ropes." Rosie O'Donnell, who first achieved recognition as a stand-up comic, admitted that early in her career she had no idea that a comedian was expected to generate her own material, and her first time at an open mike performance she took the stage and repeated verbatim a Jerry Seinfeld routine she had memorized. These stories are revealing and cute when told by celebrities who've achieved something, even if that something is little more than celebrity itself. They

have a different quality when attached to failure. The sight of Rupert, later in the movie, turning off his cassette recorder in frustration and yelling again at the unseen mother who's telling him to lower his volume, this time while he's attempting to cobble together a "demo tape," complete with canned applause, for Langford's office, is pathetic in several senses. That this child chastised by his mom is being incarnated by an actor then almost forty years old, and that the role of the mother is acted by director Scorsese's own mother, says a lot about the movie's nodes of identification, stuff that is often missed by critics who see nothing but patronizing contempt in the film's conception and treatment of Pupkin.

The Sardi's scene occurs less than fifteen minutes into the movie. Once again, as in the prior Scorsese/De Niro collaborations, we understand that the character we're looking at is trouble. But the showbiz milieu, the playing for (admittedly uncomfortable) laughs, and more, may lead us to think about the old Marx line about historical events transpiring first as tragedy (*Taxi Driver*) then as farce. But *The King of Comedy* is not quite a farce, either. (In the earliest scenes, though, it continues flirting with the idea that it might be a farce. The fantasy sequence in which Pupkin anticipates Jerry's reaction to his comedy demo tape begins with Langford pronouncing, "At least once in his life, every man is a genius. And I'll tell you something, Rupe, it's

Pupkin as he exists in his own imagination: debonair, confident, and witty.

Opposite: De Niro in an earlier comedy role, playing Mario in *The Gang That Couldn't Shoot Straight* (1971).

Following pages: Pupkin tries to woo former high school crush Rita (played by De Niro's then-wife Diahnne Abbott).

gonna be more than once in your life for you." He goes on to praise the qualities of Pupkin's comedy and gets him into a slapstick stranglehold as his praise grows more hyperbolic.)

It's kind of surprising, really, after the venting represented by *Raging Bull*, that De Niro and Scorsese would make, and for a period end their collaboration with, a movie of such concentrated, unresolved, and sometimes rather bewildering bad feeling. De Niro has not spoken much about the picture, but when he has, it appears that he went into it with simpler motivations than the finished product manifests: "I liked the script for *King of Comedy*. I liked the character and I thought it was funny. We shot it on the streets of New York and it gave us the chance to use things that we both knew were there. There's a scene in *Raging Bull* where everybody's yelling. I was yelling at my wife, she was yelling at me, people were yelling in the building, the alley. Those neighborhoods were loud. Someone yelled from the street, and I responded as Jake and the crew laughed and we kept it. We could use that kind of craziness in *King of Comedy*. One time an old lady, just a regular person, came over. I was sitting down outside the building waiting for Jerry Lewis to come out. She came over to me and started talking to me, and she said something to me. It was very cute and funny. We'd use spontaneous things like that."[66]

Anachronistic Nerd or Sociopath?

For the first time on screen (the second would be in Terry Gilliam's 1985 dystopian fantasy *Brazil*, in which De Niro appears as a balaclava-wearing insurrectionist of hilarious ineffectuality), there's a substantial Brechtian dimension to De Niro's performance, a sense of outsize caricature in which, with a few pointed exceptions, he refuses to act like a "real" person and cannot authentically respond to whoever he's talking to. This is underscored in the awkward dinner sequence between Rupert and Rita, the high school crush whom Pupkin is now pursuing again in anticipation of his triumph in usurping Langford. Rita is portrayed by Diahnne Abbott, to whom De Niro was married at the time; she played an object of Travis Bickle's unwanted attentions in *Taxi Driver* as well. In this scene, an onlooker (played by Chuck Low, who would go on to portray the hapless wig merchant/wannabe mobster Morris in 1990's *Goodfellas*) snarkily mimics Rupert from behind as he shows off his autograph book. De Niro's grandiose inattention to the woman he asks to be his "queen" is increasingly monstrous in contrast to the naturalism Abbott applies to her wary, weary character.

Pupkin's outsize dimension changes its dynamic from scene to scene, albeit not in ways that fundamentally undercut his bizarre character. (See also the way his "You know

De Niro, Comedian

Viewers of *The King of Comedy* can still get tripped up by the monologue that its kidnapper protagonist, Rupert Pupkin, performs on *The Jerry Langford Show*—his "ransom" for having abducted the talk show host played by Jerry Lewis. Is the highly problematic Pupkin actually talented? Is his spiel any good? Is he actually *funny*? The subjective nature of humor really creates a quandary here; if Pupkin's the genuine article, the viewer is expected to have to acknowledge that even while understanding his actions were/are aberrant. Or were they? The movie's coda sees Pupkin elevated to a form of stardom after a prison stint. In any event, as someone who hails from the same part of New Jersey that Pupkin jokes about, I can't be objective: the line about how if you misbehave in Clifton you get exiled to Passaic isn't bad.

De Niro's own overall competence in comedy seems to have been vindicated by the box office numbers of his recent *Fockers* films. But it's worth noting that for all the nuance his best performances show, his comic register is pretty broad. It's largely reactive, hinging on a scowl held for an uncomfortably long time, or a furrowed brow as he listens, or the slow burn to a furious reaction. It's very old school, and its screen-performer precursors were favorites among blue-collar pop-culture consumers of De Niro's generation: Leo Gorcey of the Dead End Kids, later the Bowery Boys, a stout, short-tempered, hat-wearing, semi–tough guy, and of course the comedy team of Abbott and Costello. There's also the comic character actor Edgar Kennedy, whose explosion after a slow burn was quite a bit more overtly blustery than what De Niro cooks up. But the boil itself is not dissimilar.

Interestingly enough, in the *The Gang That Couldn't Shoot Straight*, De Niro, playing a Calabrian athlete with limited English skills, does something not seen in his work before, or, frankly, since: he applies an antic sweetness and mime-type qualities that bring to mind Harpo Marx with a Beatles haircut. It's particularly fascinating in the context of the largely disastrously overstated performances that surround him.

Opposite top: Pupkin jealously guards a pay phone waiting for the hoped-for call from Jerry Langford's office.

Opposite bottom: Pupkin tries to convince Langford's assistant (Shelley Hack) that he has an appointment with the famous comedian.

Pupkin with fellow crazed fan Masha (Sandra Bernhard), with whom he plots Langford's kidnapping.

Following pages: Pupkin with date Rita at the home of an angry Jerry Langford.

what?" riposte to Langford at the end of the home invasion scene echoes Johnny Boy's telling off of Michael in *Mean Streets*.) The only time Rupert is fully humanized is in the sequence where he's desperately guarding a pay phone in a half crouch, lost and completely alone in the world, falling asleep while standing up. As if we can only sympathize with him when he's unconscious. And revived, Rupert can only jump into the awful pantomime of going up to Langford's office and acting as if he has an appointment.

The sociopathic (some might say autistic) inability to hear what people are actually saying to him reaches an apotheosis about an hour into the film. The breaking point of the Langford/Pupkin non-relationship comes after he wheedles Rita into trekking out to Langford's summer house. ("I love you. I wanna help change your life, if you just gimme a chance.") Once Langford returns from golf (summoned by his exceptionally flustered housekeepers) a blowout ensues, culminating in an immortal exchange. "Yeah, all right, so I made a mistake!" Rupert feints. "So did Hitler!" bellows Langford.

___

Working the Scenes

"In order to work with Bobby you have to make a deal with the devil," Lewis has said. "Bobby is no fool. He knows his craft. And that his craft

needs his time, it needs his gut to go for it. Marty would tell him from now until next Tuesday that Take 5 was super. But De Niro knows fucking well that if it goes into Take 12 and 14 and 15 he'll find an 'if' and an 'and.' If he does Take 20, he'll pick up a quick turn, and on Take 28, he's got lips tightening, which he never had through the first 27 takes. I watched him feign poor retention just to work a scene. I watched him literally look like he couldn't remember the dialogue. He knew the fucking dialogue. It was masterful. There's nothing he did that didn't stagger me."

Lewis continued that he was maybe staggered in a bad way by how De Niro stoked the fury of Langford's character by throwing anti-Semitic epithets at him. "And the cameras are rolling. I know Marty is getting what he wants. I know Bobby is feeding me. But for me not to be aware of two cameras and an entire crew and Bobby De Niro, throwing dialogue at me, 'Maybe the Jews were motherfuckers in the first place.' That didn't … But 'If Hitler had lived, he'd have gotten all of you cocksuckers' was the fucking trigger. He knew—the son of a bitch knew."[67] (Queried by Lawrence Grobel about "a story that [De Niro] got Lewis angry for a scene by saying anti-Semitic things just to push his buttons," De Niro responded, "I don't know if I said anything anti-Semitic, I might have said something to really bust his balls."[68])

Unconvincingly disguised and brandishing an unloaded gun, Pupkin kidnaps Langford.

Opposite: De Niro and director Martin Scorsese on the set of *Goodfellas* (1990).

Following pages: Pupkin finally realizes his dream to be a stand-up comedian.

Held in Contempt

"Everybody comes off horribly in this sequence," Pauline Kael wrote in her *New Yorker* review of the film, "Rita included—she gets even with Langford by stealing a small, perhaps valuable box from a table. […] The minds behind this picture come off the worst. They've set it all up for us: the cheerleader with no cheer left in her life; Langford, a relaxed, clear-faced child in a photograph displayed among his mementos but now puffy and implacable; and Rupert, annoyed with them both, because his attempt at pimping them fails. I hate most that detail of the petty theft; this movie reduces everybody to crud […]. [T]he possibility that our feelings might be engaged—that we might think we were at an ordinary movie—has to be stepped on."[69]

The issue of Kael's oddly proprietary attitude toward the artists she wrote about notwithstanding, she anticipates a popular notion about the film—that it holds its characters in extreme, smug contempt—while stumbling upon a truth about it. *The King of Comedy* is not an ordinary movie, in the same sense that *Mean Streets* is, at the very least, a slightly *more* ordinary movie, and in the sense that the ostensibly incoherent *Taxi Driver* and *Raging Bull* are not ordinary movies. But unlike *Taxi Driver* and *Raging Bull*, which tilt headfirst into the realms of irrationality, *The King of Comedy* strikes a purposefully uneasy balance between the emotional and the analytical (Scorsese and De Niro entered full analytical mode with 1995's *Casino*).

In *The King of Comedy*'s vision no one is innocent, and perhaps especially not the filmmakers. Once again referring to his own sense of implication, Scorsese told the critic J. Hoberman, "*The King of Comedy* is a reappraisal of my first fifteen years of making films, what it's been like. Rupert becomes a star, but for what?"[70] One does not want to read more into the fact that De Niro and Scorsese would not work together again for longer than half a decade, but still, there's a strong whiff of extra-diegetic finality inherent in the movie's extremely uncomfortable conclusion.

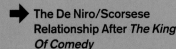

The De Niro/Scorsese Relationship After *The King Of Comedy*

"Michael Powell said about a collaboration, 'When one partner starts to get more out of it than the other, then you should break it.' Bob may not feel that way, because he might not have been aware of it. But the reality was that I wasn't as satisfied as he was," Martin Scorsese recalled in 1997. "Not because of him. He was great in *King of Comedy*. Everybody was terrific, but it didn't come from me. I said I wanted to do *The Last Temptation of Christ*; Paul Schrader wrote a terrific script, we started preparing it and then it was cancelled, totally destroyed, taken away. I was left with nothing."[e]
It's possible, too, that *Last Temptation* could have been a point of contention between the two, for De Niro had not wanted to take the part of Christ in Scorsese's proposed film.
Eight years after making *The King of Comedy* together,

the dynamic between the collaborators had changed. While Scorsese had worked consistently, he had never become a hugely "bankable" filmmaker. (His 1985 film *After Hours*, made independently on a low-budget, was an attempt to recalibrate his way of making films in the face of waning studio interest in the movies he wanted to create.) De Niro, meanwhile, had broken through into full-blown stardom, and it was his promised participation in *Goodfellas* (1990), in a part small enough to fit into his burgeoning schedule, that got Scorsese the financing for that picture. After which De Niro pulled Scorsese into the big-budget reinvention of *Cape Fear* (1991). The assets of these pictures notwithstanding, their perception was different; one did not so much have the sense of a fully revived

collaboration as of discrete special events, with De Niro doing a favor for Scorsese and vice versa. Their last collaboration to date, the mordant *Casino* (1995), also functions as a kind of dual self-portrait of men who've reached a certain age, achieved a certain level of success, and are from that point forward obliged to deal with difficult responsibilities. Since that picture was made in 1995, the professional dynamic between the men has shifted yet again: Scorsese creates big-budget, star-studded epics, while De Niro toggles between non-prestige studio projects and motley indies and hits the occasional bull's-eye, and the press periodically report a project on which the director and actor are negotiating to collaborate. If that next collaboration never happens, *Casino* can certainly stand as a sort of self-explanatory capstone.

7

Jack Walsh

Midnight Run (1988)
Martin Brest

"You know why you have an ulcer? 'Cause you have two forms of expression: silence and rage."
—Jonathan "The Duke" Mardukas (Charles Grodin)

In 1975, when De Niro was shooting *Taxi Driver*, the actor's then-agent Harry Ufland told a journalist, "Bob will never be a movie star. He is an actor. He is just not seduced by glamour."[71] By the middle of the 1980s, Ufland's prediction was still holding true. In its November 1998 issue, the New York–centric humor/satire magazine *Spy* published a piece titled "The Unstoppables," which outlined how the most talked-about actors in the culture were, by and large, not people who made movies that made a lot of money; hence, not "movie stars." This was a prime example of the damned-if-you-do-damned-if-you-don't brand of "cultural journalism" that *Spy*, for all its virtues, had a direct and aggressive hand in refining; once De Niro began to act in films that did make money, of course, he would be branded a sellout, among other things. In this particular piece, De Niro was pretty much "Exhibit A" for the case put forth by writers Rod Granger and Doris Toumarkine, which was that filmmakers who didn't succeed at providing a good return on investment needed to be punished.

The "New De Niro"

This does not mean that by the mid-eighties De Niro was at a fallow point in his career, at least as far as "the work" was concerned. Following *The King of Comedy* he appeared in another gangster epic, a movie that could not have been more different from *The Godfather Part II*: director Sergio Leone's sprawling, unstuck-in-time fantasia of brutality *Once Upon a Time in America* (1984). De Niro's work as reckless, then rueful, Jewish gangster Noodles Aaronson from late teens to old age is a protean piece of acting work, not least because, for all the character's brutality, he's essentially a recessive figure. But at the time of the film's release, its distributors, flummoxed by the movie's complex, multi-flashback structure, mutilated it, releasing a truncated, artistically bowdlerized cut that De Niro was loath to promote.

De Niro reunited with *The Deer Hunter* costar Meryl Streep for *Falling in Love* (1984), meant as a change of pace for the actor, an introduction to a more mainstream-friendly, less intense persona. Director Ulu Grosbard, the respected stage craftsman who had last directed De Niro on film in an adaptation of John Gregory Dunne's novel *True Confessions* (1981), was enthusiastic about what the picture would reveal: "a new De Niro. Nobody has ever seen this De Niro before. He's funny. He's tender."[72] But, as it turned out, nobody, or almost nobody, ended up seeing this version of De Niro; the movie did not catch on.

After a relatively small role in Terry Gilliam's *Brazil,* De Niro experimented; despite his professed lack of inclination to play roles that didn't have a kind of contemporary pertinence, he took a role in Roland Joffé's eighteenth-century period piece of Jesuits and Indians in South America, *The Mission* (1986), playing a slaver who finds faith. *The Mission* may be the most labored picture to win a Palme d'Or at the Cannes Film Festival, although De Niro's performance, which exhibits a not unconvincing soulful earnestness, is less problematic than critics who point to the movie as QED proof that De Niro can't "do" period insist.

De Niro next appeared in a supporting role in *Angel Heart* (1987), a supernatural thriller directed by Alan Parker, a director with a propensity for on-the-nose effects. For example, De Niro's part as a mysterious, powerful man who hires Mickey Rourke's detective character to go on the quest that leads to the detective's own damnation. De Niro's character (sporting a fascinating manicure, well-groomed goatee, and an orderly ponytail) is named "Louis Cyphre." That De Niro got through this role with a straight face is entirely commendable.

His subsequent work as Al Capone in Brian De Palma's *The Untouchables,* for which he gained enough weight to puff up his face but did not go to the lengths that he had in *Raging Bull*, was not just vivid in and of itself—the combination of screenwriter David Mamet's vehement, profane dialogue and De Niro in untrammeled rage mode is irresistible—but probably the most assured work he ever did for Brian De Palma, the film director with whom the actor had gotten his start on screen. As with *Angel Heart*, though, he played a supporting role. The ostensibly maverick seventies were over. Where De Niro fit into a new

De Niro as down-on-his-luck bounty hunter Jack Walsh in crime picture/buddy comedy *Midnight Run* (1988).

mode of mainstream filmmaking, one in which the achievements of the movie brats in terms of applying a sense of realism had been grafted onto the crowd-pleasing ethos of "high concept," had yet to be determined.

Agents of Fortune

By moving out of agenting and into full-time producing in 1987, the man who predicted De Niro would never be a movie star, Harry Ufland, may have forced the issue. With Ufland out, De Niro moved to the Creative Artists Agency (CAA), then led by Michael Ovitz, whose specialty was in creating optimum "packages" for his clients, as opposed to merely trying to get them cast in or assigned to potentially fulfilling projects. Said packages were, of course, more often than not replete with other CAA clients. In the case of *Midnight Run*, these included screenwriter George Gallo and director Martin Brest.

Midnight Run was a crime picture/buddy comedy of the sort refined by the 1982 picture *48 Hours*, directed by Walter Hill. The hook in this sort of picture (1987's *Lethal Weapon* is another) is that the buddies start off as antagonists and arrive at a rapprochement that's supposed to delight, and perhaps inspire, the audience. It's Neil Simon's *The Odd Couple* (1968) with guns and capers and stuff, pretty much.

De Niro has the role of Jack Walsh, a hard-bitten ex-cop and largely down-on-his-luck bounty hunter, who is, of course, looking to get out of this rotten business and open a coffee shop, if only he could make one big (and, of course, last) score. Such a score is dangled before him by a weasel-like bail bondsman, and soon Walsh has picked up Jonathan "The Duke" Mardukas, a mild-mannered accountant who's absconded with millions in mob money and donated it to charity. Everybody wants "The Duke," as it happens: the mobsters from whom he stole the money, the feds who'd like him to testify in a big case against the chief mobster, a rival bounty hunter, and so on. And "The Duke," contrary to his nickname, is hardly regal but rather plain vanilla on first meeting. But beneath his mild manner is a shrewd persnickety side that immediately abrades Walsh's streetwise bearing.

The role of Mardukas went to Charles Grodin. Eight years De Niro's senior, he was also a New York–trained stage actor. (He made his Broadway debut in the initial production of *Tchin-Tchin*, a play De Niro would perform in repertory in 1967.) While never quite achieving "movie star" status himself, he had carved out a solid film career by this time, largely playing variously uptight characters who often would not prove to be as likable as Mardukas would have to for the purposes of *Midnight Run*. (One of his most memorable awful people was the jaw-droppingly opportunistic Lenny Cantrow, who dumps his

wife mid-honeymoon to pursue a WASP beauty in Elaine May's 1972 *The Heartbreak Kid*.) Their matchup is the most inspired feature of the movie, which has arguably not aged all that well. One of the paradoxes of the picture is that the rapport between the two lead performers suffices to keep the viewer engaged despite the fact that the movie is overstuffed with scenes that really don't serve anything that could be deemed a dramatically legitimate purpose—apparently at the behest of director Martin Brest, who, fresh from the success of *Beverly Hills Cop* (1984) brought car chases, prop-plane thefts, and helicopter pursuits into what had been mostly a trains-and-autos trek.

For his part, Grodin knew from the beginning the kind of challenge working with De Niro represented; writing of the audition process in his memoir, he recalls, "the ability to improvise was one of my main assets and really the only one that might get me the role over a big movie star."[73] As their work continued, the actor discovered that their offscreen personalities did not match their roles as closely as their fans might assume. The movie's river rapids sequence relocated the movie's production to Melbourne, where Grodin found himself impressed with De Niro's ability to procure a decent meal wherever in the world he might land for work: "I was someone who had been seen in movies often playing more sophisticated, worldly people than Bob, who often played a man of the streets, known for strapping weapons to his body so that he could dispatch you unexpectedly. In fact, as I've said, in life—as a teenager anyway—I would sometimes have a knife strapped under my pants leg while making my way through rough areas. Even though it was never used, I had been a strapped-knife kind of guy. Bob (in the movies, Mr. Hidden Weapons), in life was a connoisseur—not just about where to stay, but about where to eat and drink once you got there. Somehow he would find the most elegant French restaurants hidden away in the least likely backwoods spots."[74]

Playing a Role

De Niro enters *Midnight Run* in what appears to be fighting trim. Lean but looking a little more broad-shouldered than he has in prior films, puffing away on a cigarette, he executes a daring capture of a bail jumper … but is caught out, as it were, by Marvin, a nasty, flannel-shirt-clad rival played by John Ashton (who had served a similar gruff-stout-balding-character function in *Beverly Hills Cop*). The notion of playing a role raises its head within the storyline when, backed into a situational corner by Ashton's hostile, profane Marvin, De Niro's Walsh fakes him out and, having successfully distracted him, knocks him out to bring his quarry to Joe Pantoliano's unctuous bondsman. A subsequent exchange between the two sees De Niro's character not

actually saying the words "I'm getting too old for this shit" (a mantra introduced by Danny Glover's character in *Lethal Weapon* and a subsequent addition to the lingua franca of both film and, for probably too many unfortunate souls, real life) but for all intents and purposes acting them out.

Watching De Niro in this picture with a consciousness of the movie's context at the time of its release is odd, because there's a sense of a retread involved. De Niro is now in a mainstream work that's highly informed by the tough guy tropes that he and Scorsese pioneered in the seventies. And as he'll do more explicitly in his performances in mobster or cop roles after the turn of the century, he ever so slightly mocks those conventions in *Midnight Run*. The film partakes of all the clichés of its genre, and Jack Walsh, the man of integrity working below his station (we learn that the reason he's not a cop anymore is because he refused to be corrupted by the very forces that are now out to kill Mardukas), is one of the biggest clichés of them all. What makes Walsh interesting, if he's interesting at all, is that he's being played by De Niro. But while this was the first really ordinary genre picture De Niro worked in as De Niro the Protean Actor, Hollywood by this time was full of actors who aspired to De Niro's status, acting in precisely these sorts of films. So at times in *Midnight Run* there are instances when De Niro's application of his own unique talents to the project yields results that look strangely

secondhand. (Consider a supporting player such as Pantaliano: *Mean Streets* and movies like it arguably made him viable as a type.)

The impression gains strength as the movie continues. After taking the assignment to bring in Mardukas, Walsh is accosted by a cadre of FBI agents, led by Yaphet Kotto, who dwarfs De Niro to the extent that Kotto constitutes his own special effect. Kotto's character, Alonzo Mosely, warns Walsh off his errand in no uncertain terms, and Walsh affects to be unimpressed, fake-bantering with the lawmen about their snazzy eyewear. "These sunglasses, they're really nice," Walsh coos with Rupert Pupkinesque fake sincerity. After the feds take off, we see that Walsh has pickpocketed Mosely's badge, and De Niro walks up the sidewalk, turning and "drawing" the ID fold like a gun.

Pushin' Hard Enough

It's not until Walsh tracks down Mardukas in New York, and Grodin and De Niro begin playing actorly tennis, that the movie settles into a groove that is able to distinguish it from the entirely predictable trek it still winds up being. Which is not to say that the dynamic between the actors is particularly varied. Initially Grodin underplays his character's tetchiness, affecting an air of calm resignation as Walsh cuffs him and leads him out of his cozy Manhattan town house. Befuddled by

his gentility (as we saw in the first scene, Walsh is used to preys who resist a lot more, and a lot more violently, than Mardukas does), Walsh grouses, "I know you all of two minutes and already I don't like you," to which Mardukas/Grodin replies, "Gee, that's too bad, I really like you," and Grodin's meticulous modulation is both immediately hilarious and kind of tantalizing: one does not know precisely what to make of the character.

Much of what happens subsequently in the movie seems to be conspiring to make a hash of Grodin's careful work (e.g., the completely useless detour to an Indian reservation where Mardukas, who had balked at getting on a plane with Walsh because he was afraid to fly, actually tries to take off in a prop plane after eluding his captor). De Niro's role becomes mostly reactive after he meets up with Grodin. "… here come two words for you: shut the fuck up," Walsh orders once the pair board an interstate bus, and the film's comic mileage derives from Mardukas refusing to "shut the fuck up" and Walsh's increasing exasperation as his quarry keeps on talking. But of course Walsh needs softening up, too, as per the conventions of this kind of movie.

Improvisation and Realism

It was during the shooting of one of these scenes that De Niro received a taste of his own improvisational medicine. Bear in mind the question he asked Joe Pesci from behind the camera for a confrontation scene in *Raging Bull* and his baiting of Jerry Lewis during a squirm-inspiring scene in *The King of Comedy*. Here's an account from an item in the *New York Times*: "It was understood that Mr. Grodin might have some opportunity to improvise. The 'night boxcar scene,' as Mr. Grodin calls it, was, he said, improvised entirely. The situation begins with Mr. Grodin as Mardukas shutting a boxcar door in Mr. De Niro's face in an effort to escape him. Mr. De Niro, in the role of Jack Walsh, promptly boards the car from the other side—enraged. But, Mr. Grodin said of the scene, 'We knew it had to end with De Niro revealing something personal about himself'— the history of a wristwatch that has sentimental value. 'How do you get to that point in a couple of minutes where he's going to reveal himself? What do you say?' Mr. Grodin went back to his motel and wrote down about 15 lines he thought might change the mood of Mr. De Niro, who tends to stay enraged when he becomes enraged. Back to the boxcar, with a crew of about 40 people looking on: comes the crucial moment. Mr. Grodin tries line No. 1: 'When you get your money for turning me in, you might want to spend some on your wardrobe.' 'Not a glimmer of a smile,' said Mr. Grodin. 'Nothing. [Director Martin] Brest comes over: "I love you. You've got to find a way." 'It took me ten days to get ready for Take 1,' Mr. Grodin said. 'All those people in the boxcar. It was a tough

Opposite and right: Despite all
the obstacles, Walsh still has
the Duke prisoner—in
handcuffs that were a sore
trial to actor Charles Grodin.

Following pages: Another car
written off, Walsh tries to hitch
them a ride … from Marvin.

situation. Out of desperation I said, "What could
I say to Robert De Niro to get him off the mood
he was in?" That's when, on Take 2, I asked him if
he'd ever had sex with an animal.' Mr. De Niro's
reaction is on the screen."[75]

De Niro's own insistence on realism, which saw
him riding with the Chicago police for a couple
of weeks, actually ended up taking a physical
toll on Grodin. When De Niro's character had
to haul Grodin away, there was a conference
between the actors and Brest about the terms of
Grodin's confinement. "In the picture there were
three kinds of handcuffs used—steel, rubber and
plastic," Grodin recalls. "We were walking toward
the camera, so you couldn't actually see my hands
in the shot. I suggested I just hold my hands
behind my back and not use cuffs. Marty Brest
suggested my arms would only look exactly right
if I had cuffs on—rubber ones, since they wouldn't
be seen. Bob asked if I would mind wearing the
steel cuffs. I looked at him a moment, smiled, and
said, 'Sure.' He smiled back. Neither of us knew
what the other was thinking and didn't ask."[76]

While Grodin came from a similar training
background as De Niro—he had studied with
Lee Strasberg and Uta Hagen—his philosophy
of acting was not exactly analogous to that of
his costar. But after several takes of their walk,
Grodin began to understand the advantage of
doing the "real" thing, as it were: "I could really
feel the cuffs on my skin, adding to the depth of
my performance in the scene. Bob asked again

if I minded. I said 'Not at all,' and smiled again;
so did he. I was enjoying the nonverbal repartee
between us so much, I really didn't mind the cuff
discomfort."[77] Eventually, though, the realism
became too much, particularly after a chase scene
on foot that involved scaling a wall and going
under a truck. The cuffs cut into Grodin's wrists—
in his book he claims that he still bears the scars—
and the actors had to find a different way.

Gallo's scenario is a contraption by which the
two main characters are faced with a seemingly
insurmountable obstacle course, and the movie
is constantly cutting between depictions of the
forces that are scheming to trip Walsh up. In
Chicago there are a couple of ineffectual mobsters
constantly phoning Vegas to report to their boss,
Jimmy Serrano (Dennis Farina), the mobster
both Walsh and Mardukas have a history with.
These exchanges almost invariably end with
Farina threatening to, say, "Stab you through the
heart with a fuckin' pencil." Then there are the
ineffectual bail bondsmen who don't know their
phone is being tapped by the feds, and one of
whom doesn't know that his partner is tipping off
Farina's mobsters. And then there's Mosely, who's
on the trail of Marvin, who the ineffectual bail
bondsmen have hired to relieve Walsh.

"You know why you have an ulcer?"
Mardukas says to Walsh after the film's midpoint.
"'Cause you have two forms of expression: silence
and rage." This observation could apply to a lot of
De Niro's characters, particularly Jimmy Doyle,

the driven sax player of *New York, New York*; in *Midnight Run*, the trick was to make this true for the character even as the goal was a comedic through line as opposed to a stark portrait of alienation. Maintaining that balance is most crucial for De Niro's performance at the do-or-die point at which Walsh has to decide what he's going to do with his ostensible prey.

Suppressed Rage

The film's finale, though a too-many-cooks botch in the tying-loose-ends-together department, is not ineffective, largely because it pits De Niro's Walsh against Farina's gangster, a character Walsh has several good reasons to genuinely despise. "Doesn't it bother you that another copper's fucking your wife?" Farina asks him, unctuously, pleasantly, and for the sake of the task he has to perform, Walsh takes it. He isn't Jake La Motta. "One could single out De Niro's final encounter with Farina as an example of the actor's ability to express a suppressed rage without actually exploding," the legendary critic Andrew Sarris noted in a review of the home video release of the film,[78] and he is absolutely on target. It certainly helps in this scene that his counter is Farina, the great character actor who was himself at one time a Chicago cop and hence a great observer of human behavior among aggressive types. The back-and-forth between De Niro and Farina here, while meant to be comic,

also gives a sense of two caged animals (they are, after all, in a public place) warily circling each other … and ready to defy their circumstances if their inner rages are pressed too hard.

The Returns

Whatever the ultimate value of *Midnight Run* may be, it achieved the aim of rendering De Niro bankable. The above-mentioned article in *Spy* magazine that cited De Niro as an "Unstoppable" noted, with no trace of coyness, that it was not able to cite "final rental figures for recent releases such as Robert De Niro's *Midnight Run*." Truth to tell, it did not need to; the movie's opening weekend put a substantial chink in the authors' premise. "The movie … racked up $5,518,890 its first weekend in release, putting it among the nation's top five box office hits—a select group De Niro rarely inhabits (its returns are already more than the total grosses of such De Niro films as *Falling in Love* and *True Confessions*)," reported Harry Haun in the New York *Daily News*.[79] The movie's final tally, according to the website Box Office Mojo, was $38,413,606, about $76 million today. Not blockbuster money, but a good solid hit, and a pop-culture signifier as a result.

8

Leonard Lowe

Awakenings (1990)
Penny Marshall

Leonard: "It's quiet."
Dr. Sayer: "It's late. Everyone's asleep."
Leonard: "I'm not asleep."

"If a tree falls in a forest and no one is there to see it, does it make a sound?" goes an age-old philosophical query. Robert De Niro's performance in *Awakenings* poses the question, "If a performer creates work of both meticulous simulation and soulful lyricism in a film largely invested in conventional sentimentality, does that work have an impact?" The answer most pertinent to De Niro's cachet with a mass audience, his then newly minted movie-star status, is "sort of." His portrayal of a man who is almost literally brought back to life after decades of mute immobility is one of his most scrupulous, empathetic, and ultimately unusual. It's also one of the actor's most concise portrayals, at least in terms of screen time. It's a fascinating companion piece to the other movie in which he played an important but not quite lead role: *Goodfellas*, which reunited him with director Martin Scorsese.

Celebrity Profile

Midnight Run changed De Niro's public image from that of actor's actor to movie star, and with that came a new kind of scrutiny. (He had, of course, been mentioned in the case of the drug overdose death of John Belushi in the early eighties, having visited the comic performer on the evening of his death. For years after, some accounts had De Niro "mentoring" Belushi with extra-Method advice by encouraging him to really use drugs as research for taking a role as a junkie. De Niro vehemently denied this to interviewer Lawrence Grobel: "I would never tell anybody to take heroin—or any drug—to see what it's like. Especially heroin. I would never, ever, ever. I don't know where they got that idea. Those are the kind of things that people hear and they get retold."[80]) The year of *Midnight Run*'s release, De Niro was divorced from Diahnne Abbott, to whom he had been married since 1976, the year of *Taxi Driver*. Abbott appeared with De Niro in that film, as the concession stand attendant that De Niro's Travis Bickle tries to chat up, with awkward and eventually unpleasant results. Also a singer, she performs "Honeysuckle Rose" in *New York, New York*, and of course she is Pupkin's very put-upon onetime high school crush in *The King of Comedy*. De Niro had adopted Abbott's daughter from a previous marriage, and together they had a son in 1976, Raphael.

De Niro's return to the dating pool, such as it was, had the unwelcome side effect of increasing his appearances in gossip columns, but his visibility was also going up in the Metro and Real Estate sections of various New York newspapers. It was during the time of *Awakenings* that he began making his first forays into buying property, although his initial motivations had more to do with maintaining a certain quality of life in his own backyard than with diversifying his holdings.

Awakenings, released during the Christmas season of 1990, a traditional window for Hollywood movies courting the major industry awards, was less of an event for cinephiles than was *Goodfellas*, which came out three months earlier. Scorsese's first collaboration with investigative journalist Nicholas Pileggi, the movie was based on Pileggi's book *Wise Guy*, a very nearly unprecedented account of day-to-day life in the Mafia recounted to Pileggi by Henry Hill, a New York mobster who at the time was living under a secret identity in the Federal Witness Protection Program. De Niro did not play Hill; by this point in time he was too old to play a character who ages from his twenties onward. That role was a breakout one for Ray Liotta, a fast talker with a happy-go-lucky smirk who could explode into convincing, terrifying violence at a moment's notice. De Niro took the substantial supporting role of Jimmy "The Gent" Conway, Hill's older mentor and sometimes partner in crime. Hill and Conway pull off some daring heists while trying, mostly unsuccessfully, to rein in their psychotic buddy Tommy De Vito (Joe Pesci, who played Joey La Motta in *Raging Bull*, and who very nearly walks away with the picture in a couple of jaw-dropping scenes of homicidal behavior).

"Bob had changed a lot during those [...] years since *King of Comedy*," Scorsese said of their time on *Goodfellas*. "He had started to do much more work. [... H]e would be in *Once Upon a Time in America*, which is a big epic, then *The Mission*, which is another epic, then a quick cameo in *Brazil*—continually working and experimenting with different directors, different films. So he

De Niro as Leonard Lowe, newly "awakened" from a state of paralysis and apparent dementia.

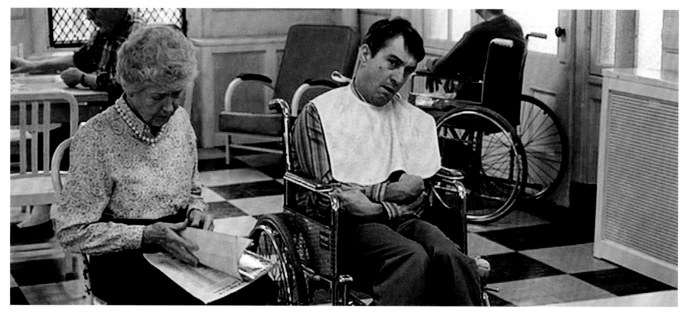

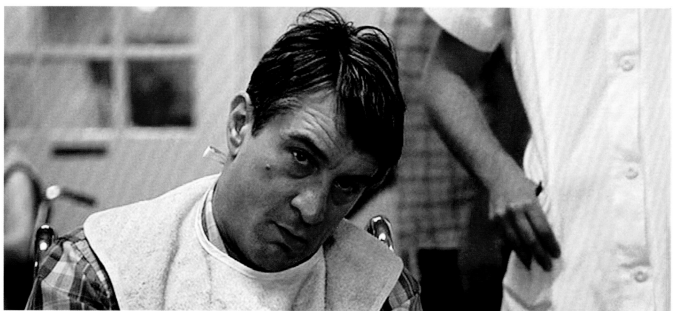

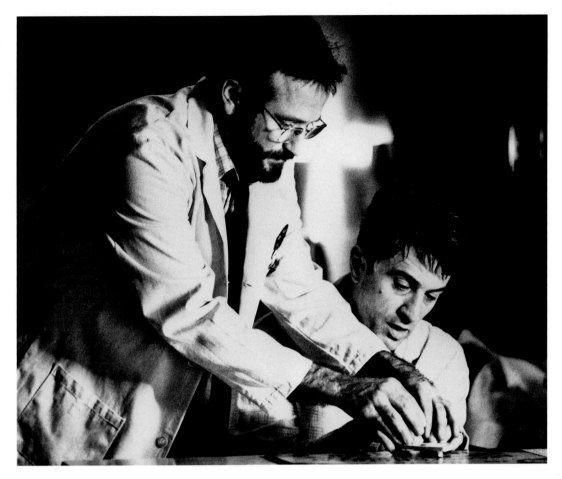

was used to working for the short time that I needed him on *Goodfellas* [De Niro was on the set for three weeks of shooting]. We had evolved a different kind of relationship. He'd just say 'What do you need?' and I would say 'I need this and that' and he'd say 'OK, let's try that.' We used to laugh sometimes in the trailer afterwards, saying, 'Do you remember years ago? We used to talk so much! What were we talking about?' I'd say 'I don't know!' It's like two people getting older. We'd start laughing, remembering the old days."[81]

Adapting and Diluting

Awakenings gave De Niro an opportunity to turn in a tour de force performance depicting a condition he had never tried to tackle before. In *Stanley and Iris* (1990) he played an illiterate man taught to read by the second title character, played by Jane Fonda. In *Awakenings* his situation would be more dire: physical paralysis and seeming catatonia, "miraculously" alleviated by the drug L-DOPA, which lifts him out of his wheelchair and into a world strange and wondrous to him and introduces him to the possibility of romance, reviving human interactions that had been lost to him since his late teens.

The movie was adapted by screenwriter Steve Zaillian from a book by Oliver Sacks, the biologist and neurologist whose medical work has gone hand-in-hand with a very productive and at times controversial literary career. *Awakenings* was Sacks's second book, and it reported on his work with a group of patients at a Bronx hospital, whose paralysis and seeming dementia turned out to have been an aftereffect of childhood encephalitis and whose extreme symptoms were cured, at least for a while, through the administration of L-DOPA. Sacks's book, after its introduction, tells twenty case histories, of which "Leonard L.," who would become Leonard Lowe, the character played by De Niro, is the last. A series of "Perspectives" follows, and ten years after the book's initial publication Sacks added an epilogue.

Its contents, of course, would be diluted in its Hollywoodization. In Leonard L.'s case, for instance, there's no trouble conveying the real person's love of literature; in his semi-paralytic state he is able to spell out, on a Ouija board, that he feels trapped like the panther in the famous poem by Rainer Maria Rilke. But Sacks's account takes on a particular kind of poignancy when the "awakened" Leonard finds a yearning for the physical love that his condition denied him turning into an urgent and increasingly irrational one. This passed, in Sacks's words, "from a gentle amorousness to an enraged and thwarted erotomania. [...] Driven at times by libidinal force, he started to masturbate—fiercely, freely, and with little concealment—for hours each day."[82] If this sort of thing was not going to play in a brutal account such as *Raging Bull*, it certainly

wasn't going to go over in this film. The movie Leonard would not be a masturbator, although De Niro's character would be allowed some earnest glances at hip-shaking young ladies in minidresses. (The movie's action is set in 1969.)

Directing *Awakenings* would be Penny Marshall, the actress and sister of television and film comedy producer/director Garry Marshall; he cast her frequently in his various successful series, and she eventually became a star on one of them, *Laverne and Shirley*. Her picture *Big* (1988) made her the first female director whose film grossed over $100 million. *Big* was a disarming modern fairy tale in which the lead character, an twelve-year-old boy, wished to become "big" and then grew into Tom Hanks. De Niro had actually been up for the role, and it's clear from some of his work in *Awakenings* that he looked at the subsequent picture as a vehicle in which to play, at least briefly, a child-man somewhat similar to the one that Hanks embodied.

The actor to play the stand-in for Oliver Sacks, in the film renamed Malcolm Sayer, was Robin Williams. A stand-up comedian and also an alumnus of a Garry Marshall series, *Mork and Mindy* (on which he played a space alien whose hyper manner was an adaptation of Williams's free-associative stand-up persona), Williams, branching out from mainstream superstardom, had been making a very credible name for himself as a "straight" dramatic actor. His work in *Dead Poets Society* (1989) had earned him his second Best Actor Oscar nomination. Still, once De Niro was cast as patient to Williams's doctor (the two share top billing in the film), there was a shift in the perceived dynamic of the movie. Sure, Williams had done great work opposite character actors and young fellows playing prep school students, but how would he fare against acting powerhouse Robert De Niro? Indeed, this question, or a variant thereof, would be reiterated time and again in subsequent years, particularly as De Niro's costars got younger and/or more ostensibly implausible (as in 1997's *Cop Land*, which played De Niro off the considerably less immediately expressive Sylvester Stallone).

The conditions under which De Niro made the deal to play in *Awakenings* speak to his expanding concerns at the time. Developers had been encroaching on Tribeca, a downtown enclave of Manhattan where De Niro had made his home. As part of his deal for *Awakenings*, the production office of that movie would be situated in a onetime coffee warehouse near the loft that De Niro had bought with a couple of other investors, now the home of De Niro's concern Tribeca Film.

***

Leonard and Malcolm

Awakenings opens in 1920s New York, conveyed with crisp authority by cinematographer Miroslav Ondříček, a Czech who also shot the handsome period films *Ragtime* (1981) and *Amadeus* (1984). Some young boys are goofing around; one of them carves his name, Leonard, into a slat of a park bench. The young Leonard (played by child actor Anthony Nici Jr.) has a mole on the right side of his face, just as the adult De Niro does in real life; this is both a signal to the audience and an acknowledgement that De Niro's particular features have entered the visual lexicon of movie stardom. A brief series of subsequent scenes recount the mysterious degeneration suffered by Leonard, who had been an A student but is suddenly unable to write his own name. Later in the movie, the ability to write one's own name becomes emblematic of a sense of self.

Williams's entry is not hugely promising. His character, a fictionalized version of Sacks, has at least one trait of Sacks himself: his shyness is, by his own account, near crippling for Sacks. In the film, it's working with patients that helps Sayer overcome that shyness. Williams's first scene, a job interview at the hospital where the action will largely be contained, has him tentative, ticky, and trying out some kind of mid-Atlantic accent. He does, however, resist the temptation to get ingratiatingly cute, a tendency that would trip up a lot of his future performances. By the time De Niro shows up in the film, Williams has found his footing.

Sayer's work with his other immobilized patients, one of whom, he discovers, can effortlessly catch a small ball thrown her way, has him delving into their supposed untreatability, and as the hospital head, played by John Heard (who portrayed a similar unpleasant skeptic in *Big*), scoffs that all Sayer is proving is that the patients still have reflexes, the viewer is meant to understand that while the authorities think Sayer is loony, he's actually a visionary. It's into this reality that De Niro's immobile Leonard Lowe is introduced. At first it is very striking indeed to see an entirely vacant De Niro. In the wheelchair he sits, hands fixed in gnarled positions, head lolling to one side, eyes looking at ... what?

Forty-six minutes into the movie, Leonard, having had no response to circumscribed doses of L-DOPA, awakes after Sayer administers a stiffer dose. Of course, Sayer falls asleep at Leonard's bedside and himself awakes to find the patient's bed empty. Leonard is sitting at a table in the next-door dayroom, trying to write out his name in crayon. He looks scared; confronted by Sayer, he gives a little smile, then a grimace; with halting speech, he observes that the room is "Quiet." There's a poetry here, something De Niro had never quite gone for before, but it's a quirky poetry. De Niro is now a middle-aged man, a little blockier, a lot less angular in his features than he was in *Taxi Driver*. There's something slightly cozy about him, but he carries a strong sense of unease. Even as he sits and looks out at the evening of his first awakening, his eyes twinkling, the actor conveys a depth of loneliness that's very different

131

from the abyss he could convey playing a nihilist such as *Mean Streets*' Johnny Boy. Not until *Stone* will De Niro again convey such an acute devotion to portraying the ages of a man.

While De Niro's performance registered well with most critics and with audiences as well, not everyone is convinced by it. David Thomson, in his *Biographical Dictionary of Film*, observes that while De Niro's work in this picture is "virtuoso," he still seems to Thomson like "Bickle trying to kid the hospital."[83] This is slightly unfair but not entirely off base. As with *Midnight Run*, there are a number of recognizable gestures and modes visible here that in later years would suffice to provide an impressionist with De Niro's greatest hits. When the L-DOPA begins to become less effective and Leonard becomes agitated and inexplicably takes over a ward full of psychotics, his preachings do call to mind Bickle's "You're in a hell! And you're gonna die in a hell!" rant in *Taxi Driver*. And the way Leonard shoos his mother away when he's trying to find a way to pursue the young woman he's seen in the hospital halls looks suspiciously like Jimmy Conway's gesture to Henry Hill's wife late in *Goodfellas* as he tries to steer her into what would be doom should she take his direction.

Nevertheless, the performance has many wonderful things in it, stuff we have not seen De Niro do before. While still caught up in the euphoria of his mobility, Leonard has a sudden realization that the viewer's not privy to until he runs to the mirror to confirm it: that, yes, he is much older than he had thought he was. These moments are strengthened by the excellent work of the supporting cast playing Leonard's fellow patients. Several of these actors are veterans of the New York stage and had training similar to De Niro's. One of them, Judith Malina, was herself a major theater innovator in New York, a cofounder of the Living Theatre. She had been a student of the radical dramatist Erwin Piscator, whose wife was a client of De Niro's mother and through whom De Niro first began auditing classes at Piscator's Dramatic Workshop. Then there's Dexter Gordon, the legendary jazz saxophonist who made a striking acting debut at age sixty-three in Bertrand Tavernier's 1986 movie *'Round Midnight* (for which he got a Best Actor Oscar nomination) and who here strikes an odd, somewhat feminized gait as his awakened character speaks mostly through music. The scenes in which these performers enact the elation and then the oddness of their newfound mobility often achieve a sustained lyricism that one normally never expects from this sort of picture, and De Niro's affinity with the key these performers operate in is palpable.

Also worth noting is Ruth Nelson, who gives a strong performance as Leonard's mother, whose joy at his revival is soon tempered by her own denial that her boy is not a child anymore. Nelson was a founder of the Group Theatre in New York

Given the actor's shyness, reticence as a public figure, and seeming inarticulate nature, it's difficult to picture what De Niro would be like as a director. But the job was one that he had wanted for a long time, and he had entertained writing ambitions as well; according to Paul Schrader, before they worked together on *Taxi Driver*, De Niro had been writing a script with similar themes, involving a potential assassin. Chazz Palminteri, a writer and performer only a few years De Niro's junior, had been struggling for years when he conceived and created the play *A Bronx Tale* as a vehicle for himself, playing all of its parts as a one-man show. Jane Rosenthal, De Niro's partner in Tribeca Film, recommended the show to De Niro, and Palminteri got a big break in two ways: De Niro not only decided to adapt the play as his film

directorial debut but also gave Palminteri the key role of Sonny, the gangster with a seductive lifestyle who's trying to bring young Calogero Anello under his wing. De Niro plays Calogero's bus driver father, Lorenzo, who's trying to keep his son on the right path. As much as the piece was directly autobiographical for Palminteri, it held strong resonances for De Niro as well. "When I was about 13," John Baxter quotes De Niro as saying, "[my father and I] ran into each other in Washington Square Park. I was with a group of street kids, and he got fairly worked up, going on and on about bad influences."[f] De Niro dedicated *A Bronx Tale* to his father, who died in 1993, the year of its release. While ostensibly a fictionalized historical tale, *The Good Shepherd* (2006) also deals with flawed

fathers and sons and has a particularly harrowing plot turn that provides an extremely disturbing instance of what one might call parental interference. In both these films De Niro shoots and edits in a straightforward, no-nonsense style, hardly as virtuosic in terms of visual polish and pacing as Scorsese's. He gets superb work out of his actors, which is to be expected. Although in the current climate of Hollywood it's unlikely that a project such as *The Good Shepherd* would even get made without a figure with De Niro's clout getting behind it, the actor's films as a director are not so entirely distinctive that one is necessarily clamoring for the next.

in the 1930s, and played a major role in the first production of Odets's *Waiting for Lefty*—the play that De Niro drew from when he auditioned for Brian De Palma, Wilford Leach, and Cynthia Munroe back in the early sixties, going for a role in *The Wedding Party*. Nelson went on to work with Elia Kazan on his film debut, *A Tree Grows in Brooklyn* (1945). A victim of the HUAC-inspired Hollywood blacklist along with her husband, John Cromwell, her filmography breaks off in 1948, not to pick up again until 1977. De Niro's interactions with Nelson are largely the most tender, subtle, and intuitive in the entire movie.

Leonard and His Time

De Niro's screen time is relatively short, and while there are many aspects of his and, more particularly, Williams's characters that dissolve into cliché as the movie continues (the "compassionate" way Williams gazes at his charges, how he takes on the bad feelings of his patients and tries to buck them up; these look ahead not just to his work in *Good Will Hunting* [1997] but also to the dire *Patch Adams* [1998]), De Niro does a remarkable job of maintaining Leonard's dignity even as his physical state degenerates.

The not-quite romance between Leonard and Penelope Ann Miller's character, Paula, the daughter of a stroke victim who Leonard meets while she's visiting her father, does not get very far at all, but it's crucial and provides the movie with a subtext that the movie's surface sentiments shy away from. Leonard L. is, like Travis Bickle, trying to "be a person," but his experience in immobility makes him painfully aware not just of the time behind him but of the limited time in front of him, and he of course lives in terror of returning to his former state. Without having recourse to portraying the real-life Leonard's erotomania, De Niro nonetheless, through eye movements and concentrated bouts of fidgeting, conveys Leonard's impatience even as he acts, for the sake of Paula, the old-school gentleman.

And then as the treatment begins to become less effective, the sense of loss that De Niro conveys even as Leonard's condition is threatening to turn him into (his words) "not a not a person anymore, just a collection of tics" is remarkable. Still the avid researcher, De Niro, according to Sacks, spent "hundreds of hours with patients, and at a very deep level, beyond words," sitting thirty-six hours straight with one patient to observe his symptoms rather than having them enumerated for him.[84] What De Niro brings as the movie requires him to rein Leonard back into a realm of blankness goes far beyond mimicry. Despite the occasional false note the movie strikes (most glaringly, the complicit smile between Sayer and Leonard as the other

patients come back to life), what registers most strongly in De Niro's performance are ineffable senses of both what's given to the character and what's taken away from him. This is a feat not merely of technique but of empathy.

The movie itself almost buries this in its finale, with its requisite speech from Williams's character about how "the human spirit is more powerful than any drug." In a way, this is not entirely inapt, because what resonated with viewers about De Niro's performance was not, it would seem, its nuances, but the way that he came off as almost cuddly in the midsection scenes of Leonard, in his anachronistic bow tie, going out into the world and doing all manner of "the wonder of life" activities. *Awakenings* succeeded where the likes of *Falling in Love* and *Stanley and Iris* had failed: it gave audiences a credible De Niro over which to become sentimental.

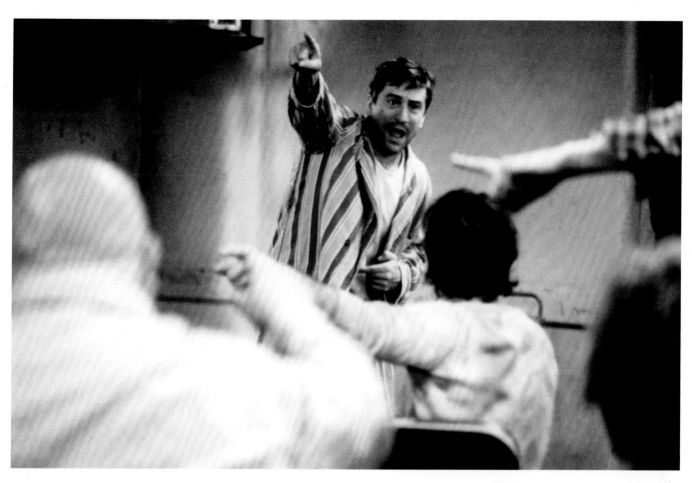

9

Jack Byrnes

Meet The Parents (2000)
Jay Roach

"I mean, can you ever really trust another human being, Greg?"
—Jack Byrnes

The decade separating this film from *Awakenings* represented for many De Niro watchers, professional and otherwise, a dispiriting dismantling of his myth. His filmography from 1991 to 1999 sees De Niro appearing in more than twenty films. A close look at the filmography reveals a not insubstantial number of high points. But these mingle with misfires, most of them appearing to be good faith efforts that didn't work out. *Guilty by Suspicion* (1991) and *Night and the City* (1992), for instance, were fledgling directorial efforts from veteran producer Irwin Winkler, who had been behind *Raging Bull* and *The King of Comedy* with director Martin Scorsese; both fizzled.

De Niro in the 1990s: A Very Mixed Bag

De Niro made his own directing debut with the affecting urban parable *A Bronx Tale* (1993), in which he also gave a solid performance as a working-class dad. Also outstanding in its understatement was his performance in *Mad Dog and Glory* (1993), a lightly quirky tale of a romantic misunderstanding precipitated by a meeting between a shy cop and an odd mobster who aspires to be a stand-up comic, featuring Bill Murray and Uma Thurman.

One key to understanding the differing choices De Niro made during this period lies in a statement he made in an interview to promote *This Boy's Life*, a picture he made in 1993 (and one that featured a young Leonardo DiCaprio, who would go on to a series of collaborations with Martin Scorsese). "When I was younger, I might have been more obsessive about preparing for a role like Dwight. But that could be too much of an energy drain. Now I'm more relaxed and approach things moment to moment ... I guess when you're older and more experienced, you see what's important."[85] In the movies of this period in which De Niro's performances have had the most effect, the critical viewer can detect something different from the absolute immersion that characterized his work in *Taxi Driver* and *Raging Bull*. The emphasis seems less on the idea of "becoming" the character than in identifying and nailing defining or transformative moments for the character.

There were exceptions, of course. The two films director Martin Scorsese made with De Niro during this period were both extremely violent crime dramas, but in all other respects could not have been more different from each other. After the relative success of *Goodfellas*, a box office hit if not a record-breaking smash, Scorsese undertook a remake of the dark late-fifties thriller *Cape Fear*, with De Niro in the role of vengeful ex-convict Max Cady. Scorsese's determination to explore, in Cassavetes-style depth, the internal tensions of the family Cady victimizes (portrayed by Nick Nolte, Jessica Lange, and Juliette Lewis) abraded oddly against the polished blockbuster surfaces of the film. As did the extremes the film went to in portraying Cady's depredations. *Casino* (1995), like *Goodfellas* an adaptation of a nonfiction account by Nicholas Pileggi, had De Niro playing Sam "Ace" Rothstein, a gambling maven who, through the good graces of the Kansas City mob, gets to run his own Vegas joint his own way, for about ten minutes at least, until crazy gangster associates and bad romantic choices gum things up. This lengthy, extremely detailed picture is one of Scorsese's most intellectual. Unlike his seventies pictures, with or without De Niro, it holds its characters at a kind of analytical remove. The agonized metaphysics animating the likes of *Taxi Driver* and *Raging Bull* are here replaced by a bracing materialist critique of capitalism within meta-movie tropes.

Other highlights of this De Niro decade include his first face-off with Al Pacino, in another epic crime picture, Michael Mann's *Heat*; a galvanic turn as an abusive stepdad in *This Boy's Life* (1993); a flexing of the action-movie chops in *Ronin* (1998); and two sides of the same coin, in a comic sense: a couple of very dry, canny performances in extremely unrelated pictures of 1997. In *Wag the Dog*, an amusing, albeit highly facile political satire concocted by writer David Mamet and director Barry Levinson, De Niro plays Conrad Brean, an eccentrically dressed, cynical-avuncular political consultant who ropes a Hollywood

De Niro as the nightmare father-in-law-to-be, former CIA agent Jack Byrnes.

producer, played by Dustin Hoffman, into faking a war for the sitting president. De Niro underplays splendidly as he flatters Hoffman's Stanley Motss into steamrolling all ethical considerations in the name of patriotism and show business, and then shows no hesitation when a situation calls for him to curb Motss's enthusiasm for self-promotion with extreme prejudice. In contrast, his ex-con Louis Gara in *Jackie Brown*, writer-director Quentin Tarantino's adaptation of an Elmore Leonard novel, is a dead-eyed, grunting, no-souled simpleton, but a relatively good-natured one, or so it seems, until another character's pushing him too far results in his lethal acting-out. Because *Jackie Brown* is the better film, De Niro's funny-until-it-isn't performance has more impact, but his actual work in *Wag the Dog* is just as meticulously calibrated.

But for all that, the pattern one sees beginning in certain films indicates worse to come. For example, *Backdraft* (1991), an overlong all-star firefighting saga directed by Ron Howard, featured De Niro in a role that was pretty much the inverse of his purposeful *Goodfellas* supporting character, that of an arson investigator whose ostensible expertise serves no function except to afford De Niro the opportunity to break out a gallery of tics: this particular grimace, that particular brow-furrow, a slightly hunched-over stance to signal above-average levels of concentration, and so on.

De Niro and …

A salient feature of the (largely) lesser De Niro movies of this period was what I'll call the "De Niro and" factor. Its roots were in the unsuccessful (in box office terms) pairing of De Niro and Streep in *Falling in Love*, more or less duplicated by the pairing of De Niro with Jane Fonda in *Stanley and Iris*. As De Niro approached his fifties, and the influence he had exerted on a younger generation of actors (including Sean Penn, whose working method on his early films was similar in its character-immersion to De Niro's) became clear, pairing De Niro with those younger performers became an ostensible draw. But through the nineties, and arguably beginning with *Awakenings*, the concentration was on pairing him with performers who were not too far from him in age but dissimilar in terms of the associations they carried. Hence, dryly comic actor Bill Murray in *Mad Dog and Glory*; the formal, Olivier-gene-carrying (in terms of public perception at least) British actor-director Kenneth Branagh in *Mary Shelley's Frankenstein* (1994), a garish disaster in which Branagh played the scientist, and De Niro amplified the symptoms of *Awakenings*' Leonard to portray the atavistic creation;

Stallone in *Cop Land* (1997); schticky and then still mildly ingratiating comic Billy Crystal in *Analyze This* (1999).

De Niro Still Doesn't Play Joy

It is De Niro the cartoon (arguably first seen in 1996's *The Fan*, in which De Niro's character catapults out of regular-guy-with-issues mode into a middle-aged Looney Tunes iteration of Travis Bickle/Rupert Pupkin) who turns up in *Meet the Parents*, a comedy whose semiotics may be more interesting than its scenario. The film is De Niro's first comedy without an action or crime element driving the plot. It is true that in *Meet the Parents* De Niro's character Jack Byrnes is revealed to be a retired CIA agent, but this plot point is used more as a way to misdirect the character Gaylord "Greg" Focker, played by Ben Stiller, than as a defining aspect of the character.

As has become more common in American studio-made comedies in (at least) the last decade, particularly comedies driven by sensibilities rooted in improv and sketch, Jack Byrnes has no real defining aspects aside from the particular kind of stern quasi-menace of which De Niro is a master. He exists not as a thing itself, but merely as an object to touch off massive discomfort in the ostensible hero of a romantic-comedy quest. However, he is a formidable, intimidating, maybe even immovable object. The whole point of making De Niro into a terrifying potential father-in-law is that he's De Niro, the onetime lethal and thoroughly cool seventies antihero. While De Niro might not have approached his earlier roles with the purpose of being somewhat misunderstood as far as icon status goes, in the latter part of his career he's comfortable with satirizing that, even if it takes him into realms that critics will condemn as self-parody.

In his almost unremittingly hostile biography of De Niro, John Baxter recounts the unfortunate encounter between De Niro and Mike Nichols, the film and stage director and occasional performer who tried to direct De Niro in *Bogart Slept Here* (1977), from a script by *The Odd Couple* writer Neil Simon. The association lasted all of two weeks. By Baxter's account, "Nichols was reported as saying 'This man is undirectable,' and that De Niro 'simply wasn't funny.' Simon conceded 'Robert De Niro is a very intense actor. He doesn't play joy well.'"[86] Later Baxter insists, "*Midnight Run* was a cruel lesson in what Mike Nichols had said at the time of *Bogart Slept Here*—he simply wasn't funny."[87] The subjective nature of successful comedy notwithstanding, popular opinion does not hold with Baxter's verdict. And, as it happens, his inability or disinclination to "play joy" also notwithstanding, De Niro has been very funny in a number of movies that, admittedly, are not

frequently noted for their comedic content. The ingenuousness of Bruce Pearson sometimes induces laughter. The "Joey Clams/Joey Scala/ same guy" back and forth between Keitel and De Niro in *Mean Streets* actually does register as good schtick; and as terrifying as Johnny Boy's climactic "I borrow money from everybody" soliloquy at that movie's climax is, it's suffused with mordant hilarity.

Jack's Big Moment

There's a De Niro moment in *Meet the Parents* that makes me laugh as reliably as the "I borrow money from everybody" schtick in *Mean Streets* does. It's shortly after the largely hapless male nurse Greg Focker, played by Stiller, is introduced to Jack Byrnes, who Focker believes is a retired exotic florist. Jack is telling Greg about a business venture he's started to keep himself busy in retirement. By way of a preface, Jack asks, "I mean, can you ever really trust another human being, Greg?"

The dynamic that's already established is that Greg is walking on eggshells. His initial attempt at proposing to Pam (Teri Polo) was scotched after he learned that the fellow marrying Pam's sister asked Jack's permission first. So, Greg has reengineered his proposal plans so as to include the asking-for-Pam's-hand into his process. To this end, he has packed an engagement ring into

the luggage he's taking on a Chicago-to-New York flight to attend the relatively impromptu wedding of Pam's sister to "Dr. Bob." That piece of luggage is checked, and lost. This is one of the first in a series of, plausibility note-takers of films will insist (and not without reason), entirely avoidable mishaps for Greg, the significance of which is only exacerbated by Jack's suspicious nature. So, the question "Can you ever really trust another human being?" is in some respects fraught. It's here that, Stiller deftly conveys in his performance, Greg considers whether to say what he actually believes and then decides, yes, that's what he's going to do. And he answers, with no little sincerity and resolve, "Sure. I think so."

And here De Niro calibrates his forward-lean, brow-furrow, and slight headshake in perfect sync with a slightly flat but very definite delivery of "No. The answer is you cannot." This by way of introducing a new security device of his invention, a variant on the babysitter monitoring "Nanny Cam." The line "No. The answer is you cannot" is nothing special, but the delivery, which is not overtly contemptuous but nonetheless hammers home the sense that Greg might as well not have opened his mouth at all, is remarkable, and hilarious. If the character's subsequent bits of business had remained within these lines, the performance would have stayed, possibly, as funny.

Bonding (or Not) with Greg

What follows immediately is not awful: after receiving a phone call, Jack runs out on what the audience knows is a made-up errand, and Pam and her mom, Dina (Blythe Danner, whose character is as messy as Jack's; sometimes she plays relatively competent confidante and helpmeet, other times she reacts to events like she's just coming out of electroshock), encourage Greg to tag along for bonding practice, despite the fact that Jack really needs to go out alone. In the car there are many awkward pauses between Greg and Jack. Jack, who dotes on his toilet-trained Himalayan cat "Mr. Jinx," quizzes Greg on his "dog-person"-hood, saying, "You prefer an emotionally shallow animal." This is pretty good stuff as it goes. Jack puts on the car audio system and begins singing along with Peter, Paul, and Mary's "Puff the Magic Dragon." The calculation is not so different as when, in another era of moviemaking, MGM announced "Garbo Laughs!" *Meet the Parents* mines comedy out of showing De Niro as audiences have rarely if ever seen him before: singing! And not just singing, but singing along to a dippy sixties folk song! (Of course, as we've seen, De Niro had sung on-screen at least once before: in *Bang the Drum Slowly*. Then again, that's a movie that *Meet the Parents*' "key demo" is not that likely to know well.)

This establishes a pattern that the movie defaults to more frequently as it ratchets up the physical humor. The continuation of Greg's misadventures in Jack-approval seeking makes the characters cogs in quasi-screwball-comedy set pieces engineered by a Rube Goldberg with a taste for toilet humor. As when Pam's of course wildly successful ex-fiancé attempts to deliver a hand-carved altar to the Byrnes' backyard just as their house's septic tank is overflowing and its contents are seeping up into the lawn, and we see Robert De Niro as we've never seen him before: getting splattered in fake liquefied excrement! The actor is certainly game for this (and we in the audience are all reasonably sure that De Niro, his former penchant for absolute realism notwithstanding, is not in any kind of biohazard danger), but unless one's sense of humor is directly attuned to such fare, the most one can muster as a reaction to this is admiration for his being a good sport and/or professional.

Similarly overdetermined is the schmuckiness of Greg's character. On the other hand, for De Niro fans who are more invested in the actor than the movie surrounding him, the actor's reactions can be a kind of saving grace, particularly when they occur during the schticky Stiller bits. Stiller's character is meant to be a "mensch" in ways that offset his haplessness plausibly enough that the audience can understand how Pam fell in love with him. But the haplessness is often overplayed, as in Greg's first dinner at the Byrnes', during which he's asked to give a benediction, or "say grace." Pam protests that as Greg is Jewish, he's not properly equipped to do so. But Greg counters, of course he can. Whereupon he launches into a ramble in which he thanks the Lord for the "smorgasbord" in front of him and stumbles into a recitation of the lyrics of "Day by Day," a song from the 1970s Jesus-musical *Godspell*, which he had heard on the sound system of a store in a prior scene. Whether you find it funny or not, the sequence simply does not parse, unless you reconfigure conventional cinema space to the dimensions of a comedy club. De Niro's raised eyebrows remain stalwart as Stiller goes off the rails.

De Niro evinces similar performance integrity in a later scene whose contents might prove frustrating to those who put the actor in their personal pantheon of tough guys. After Pam's stoner brother Denny lies to Jack about a pot pipe of his, telling his dad it belongs to Greg, Jack dresses down Greg, who he's only just admitted into the Byrne family's "circle of trust," and tells him that if he violates that trust, "I will bring you down, baby. I will bring you down to Chinatown." This, of course, is an amusingly absurd riff on the warning Al Pacino's character gives to De Niro's in the crime drama *Heat* (to which De Niro then gives Pacino the "flip side" comeback), made only five years before. For certain of De Niro's detractors, the bit might play as a particularly bitter "betrayal," sacrificing badassdom on the altar of cheap laughs.

Self-development

It might have been less bitter for them had De Niro himself not been the direct author of such desecration. Because the most salient feature of *Meet the Parents* is not so much De Niro's participation as a performer but as a producer. De Niro's forays into film production began coming about around the same time that he went in on the purchase of what would become the Tribeca Film Center. He created a production company also called Tribeca. It's not uncommon for actors to set up their own production companies. Humphrey Bogart did it back in the fifties. Among other things, it was a convenient entity in which to pour money one did not want to be taxed on, but De Niro was not looking for a mere write-off. On the recommendation of Martin Scorsese, he hired a fresh, eager onetime executive named Jane Rosenthal, and got her to work on a slate of potential films. More than anyone else, Rosenthal has been the central figure in De Niro's professional life since that time.

Meet the Parents began its life as a 1992 short cowritten by and starring Greg Glienna and Mary Ruth Clarke, who have subsequently been credited on all three *Parents/Fockers* films as creating their main characters. It was developed into a feature-length picture by screenwriters John Hamburg and Jim Herzfeld, and after Universal/

Intimidation, threats, and veiled accusations from Jack as he believes Greg to have broken the Byrnes family circle of trust.

Dreamworks attached Jay Roach, who had substantial success with the *Austin Powers* spy-parody films cocreated by Mike Myers, to direct, Rosenthal lobbied hard to get De Niro into the Byrne role and by dint of that became one of the movie's coproducers.

John Baxter's account of the making of the film sets it up for failure. Summing up the shoot, he writes, "The result looks like a film capable of making a modest profit. But De Niro's fee and the complicated physical action pushed the budget to $55 million—more than the cost of any similar film."[88] As he recounts this, Baxter is aware of the happy ending, and it comes a couple of pages later: "As the October release date of *Meet the Parents* approached, De Niro can have had few reasons to be optimistic. Yet the film grossed more than half its budget on the first weekend, the biggest October opening in Hollywood history, and built into one of the year's most profitable productions. 'Who would have imagined,' asked Jane Rosenthal, with understandable surprise, 'that Bob De Niro would turn out to be America's funniest man?' Universal and Dreamworks immediately offered Jim Herzfeld $1.1 million to script the sequel, *Meet the Fockers*."[89]

A biographer who seems to regret the fact that he cannot accuse De Niro of having run a Soviet gulag, Baxter of course makes it look as if De Niro and Rosenthal succeeded here through sheer luck. Given the subsequent success of dozens of comedies not necessarily starring De Niro but very much in the *Meet the Parents* social-discomfort mode—material such as the two 2005 movies *The Wedding Crashers* (costarring Owen Wilson, who also appears in *Meet the Parents*) and *The 40-Year-Old Virgin*, immediately spring to mind—one could argue more credibly that they were prescient.

"I'm Bob De Niro"

De Niro's investment in the picture was such that he agreed to participate in what had become a de rigueur exercise for a film's "talent": he sat in a recording studio for the DVD audio commentary. His lack of comfort is almost humorously clear as he introduces himself: "I'm Bob De Niro." He then settles back into silence as Stiller, Roach, and Rosenthal talk among themselves. Roach soon tries to draw De Niro out. As his character picks up the cat, Roach says, "You always seem to really like these cats, Bob. Was that just acting, or did you actually have a connection?"

"Well, I like animals, I like cats," De Niro replies hurriedly.

"Were you able to keep track of which of the three cats you were working with each time?"

"I thought we only had two."

So it goes. Rather incredibly, Roach asks De Niro if he's had training in improvising ("Well, I've done movies where we've improvised, a bit,

you know, so …" De Niro replies) and whether he's done a lot of work in the theater. In a scene in which a cat is unsure about remaining in De Niro's lap, Roach observes, "You seemed to like having that cat a lot, Bob," and De Niro replies, "Yes. It seemed right to have the cat as much as possible."

Meet the Parents ends with another staple of the contemporary rom-com, the airport don't-get-on-that-plane scene, after Greg's expulsion from the Byrne homestead. Greg finally asserts himself, but in a not-constructive way, insisting on marching onto the plane with his oversize piece of luggage and launching into an enraged tirade at a snooty flight attendant. "The airlines weren't too happy about you going off on her that much," Roach observes on the commentary track. One of the ways Stiller's character "goes off" is by mock-protesting that he's obviously not carrying a bomb in his luggage; he then starts chanting, "Bomb bomb bomb bomb bomb bomb." And again here, Roach and Stiller marvel that the film was salable to airlines at all. The DVD release of the film was March 6, 2001. In six months, films in which put-upon characters get laughs by flipping out and making loud pronouncements about bringing bombs onto airplanes would be made obsolete. And the events of 9/11 would have some very specific, direct effects on De Niro and his career.

10

Jack Mabry

Stone (2010)
John Curran

"Just go ahead and burn your motherfuckin' life up … Just embrace it, man."
 —Gerald "Stone" Creeson (Edward Norton)

As he entered his fifth decade as a film actor, Robert De Niro, always an uncomfortable public figure, had continued to succeed in keeping his name out of gossip columns and celebrity magazines. Yes, his proximity to the death of John Belushi had raised some celebrity journalists' eyebrows, as did the more tabloid-prominent women he dated after his divorce from first wife Diahnne Abbott (Toukie Smith—with whom De Niro had twins—and Naomi Campbell were both fashion models). But there wasn't much else. So a feature in *People* magazine titled "Goodfella? Badfella?" with the subhead "De Niro's estranged wife accuses him of drug use in a nasty custody battle" was a life/career twist to give an observer pause. De Niro's second marriage, to Grace Hightower, looked to have gone south in a particularly unpleasant way, and it seemed like their conflict would not be resolved anytime soon. The issue of *People* in which that article appeared was dated September 10, 2001. The next day, it's a safe bet to say that very few people in the world, even De Niro and Hightower themselves, were primarily concerned with the state of the marriage, a marriage that they were subsequently able to repair and which endures to the time of this writing.

"Whether in his posh office—where the coat rack displays an NYPD jacket and an FDNY baseball cap—or at home, De Niro encounters Ground Zero every day," Stephen Garrett wrote in a profile of the actor in *Time Out New York* in 2002. "His resulting desire to contribute to the neighborhood's ongoing recovery is intense. 'Helping out is the least you can do,' he says."[90] With Jane Rosenthal and her husband, real estate investor Craig Hatkoff, De Niro cofounded the Tribeca Film Festival in 2002. The initial idea for the event was to revitalize the traumatized and economically struggling neighborhood. In addition to this and other "giving back" efforts, De Niro continued expanding his real estate investments. While he was successfully treated for prostate cancer in late 2003, the new De Niro managed to get through this ordeal with a modicum of privacy.

A Profile to Fit His Time

In the midst of all this activity, De Niro's profile as a performer changed further. The critic Terrence Rafferty intuited that De Niro was merely adapting to his times, and to an industry for which the incredible artistic outpouring of the 1970s and early 1980s was an anomaly, a blip, rather than an indication of a lasting transformation: "It's tempting to see this actor's metamorphosis as an allegory of the changes in American film from the adventurous 70s to the craven, risk-averse 21st century. But let's not go there. For one thing, it's too depressing: in this direction lies, perhaps, a Travis Bickle–like homicidal madness. Besides, Mr. De Niro happens to be a very, very good comic actor, and if making audiences laugh is the best means he can find, in this dismal movie-making climate, to practice his art with some measure of satisfaction, then so be it. Laughs are always welcome."[91]

Laughs, cheap and otherwise (*Showtime*, De Niro's 2002 teaming with onetime comedy sensation Eddie Murphy, proved something of an embarrassment to both performers) were not the only things on De Niro's professional plate in the post-9/11 decade. The laughs did, arguably, compel critics to undervalue his serious, ambitious work, which admittedly came to screens at a slower pace. The actor's second directorial effort, *The Good Shepherd*, a fictionalized backstory of the Central Intelligence Agency, was a sprawling, solemn, deeply pessimistic story that, like De Niro's prior movie as director, *A Bronx Tale*, had a father-son story as its emotional fulcrum. De Niro acquitted himself credibly in *What Just Happened* (2008), a largely fictionalized Barry Levinson–directed adaptation of producer Art Linson's memoir. And he worked effectively in understated sentimental mode in *Everybody's Fine* (2009), as a widower reconnecting with his adult children.

But it was in *Stone* that he showed, with full commitment, the De Niro willing to go out on a limb artistically by doing the interior work of burrowing inside a character. As in several of his films of the 1970s, he plays an emotionally troubled and in many ways closed-off man. But this is a portrait of emotional and existential disturbance in old age. *Taxi Driver* ends with the ticker reset on human time bomb Travis Bickle. *Raging Bull* ends with its title character having

De Niro as the parole officer handling Stone's case, the enigmatic Jack Mabry.

achieved a mysterious peace. *Stone* begins and ends with the buzzing of a wasp and a man, at two stages of his life, alone, hearing it.

Tuning Forks

The opening scene of *Stone*, directed by John Curran from a script by Angus MacLachlan, who'd originally created the piece as a stage play, is set in the living room of a rural house on a hot afternoon. A man is sitting in a chair, watching golf on a television set. We can tell from the shape of the set and its black-and-white picture that the scene is set in the past. The man in the chair has close-cropped hair; the mole on his cheek indicates the character's identity. A young woman with red hair, who'd previously carried a little girl upstairs and into the bedroom, comes into the living room and announces to the man, her husband, that she's leaving him. "You keep my soul in a dungeon," she tells him. The man responds by going to the upstairs bedroom, opening its window, and holding the sleeping girl, their daughter, outside of it. "If you leave me I'll throw her. You think that I won't, hmm? … Do you think I won't?" he says, with rather eerie calm. That settles the argument. The man puts the girl back on the bed and shuts the window; the underside of its frame kills the wasp that has been buzzing insistently on the soundtrack throughout the scene.

The movie shifts to the present day, and we see, of course, that the young man with the mole on his cheek (Enver Gjokaj is the actor) has grown up to become Robert De Niro's character, Jack Mabry. Mabry works at a Detroit-area prison for the warden's office, interviewing and assessing candidates for parole, and he seems settled into a routine of competence and rectitude. He listens to Christian talk radio as he drives to work; he is calm as he checks his sidearm at the prison gate and organized as he files his paperwork.

As conservatively, as sanely, as Jack conducts his current affairs, of course, we can't stop thinking about the young man who held his daughter out the window. And of course we take note of the pinched, drawn face of Jack's wife (played in the contemporary scenes by Frances Conroy) and are compelled to watch Jack extra carefully as he delivers a eulogy to his late brother. It doesn't solve anything. At first Jack reads from his remarks stiffly, and the reflex reaction is to condemn his insincerity, but then his face contorts in real pain, and perhaps guilt, and the comforting easy answer about Jack dissipates.

Mabry's Last Case

Then, into Jack's office strides a presence that shifts viewer focus off of Jack for a while, so startling and odd it appears. Mabry's last case,

for the purposes of this story, is Gerald Creeson, who calls himself "Stone" for reasons he's not good at articulating. Something about his street name. Stone is quite a sight: a white man of slight build, his arms festooned with tattoos, he's got his hair in tight cornrows more common in African-American stylings and still a bit anachronistic for all that. He drawls in a painful-sounding high-pitched rasp, and the things that come out of his mouth are off-putting. After a very rocky start with Mabry, at which meeting Mabry has to lay out what the interview process is for ("We talk. We're not friends, but just pretend we're friends, okay?"), Stone settles in and answers Mabry's questions. Is Creeson married? Yes, he married one year before he was sent to prison on an arson and accessory to murder charge. And he misses his wife, he says. "She visit you much?" Mabry asks. "Picnics most Saturdays?"

"I don't want no picnic, man, I miss my dick in her fuckin' ass," Stone replies. "I miss her suckin' me till I can't take no more. I mean, she's crazy. She'll do anything. You know. Fuck her tits, come in her face, she just blink and keep on laughing … gonna give you some pictures in your head will keep you up at nights, man." Mabry stares at Stone. His little soliloquy has a bit of an echo of the spiel Harvey Keitel's Sport gives to De Niro's Bickle in *Taxi Driver*, describing what Bickle could do with the pimp's underage prostitute Iris. But the meta-moment dissipates in the genuine discomfort De Niro conveys. Norton's Stone picks up on this and begins goading him, asking how older guys like him keep their sex lives going.

According to De Niro's costar Edward Norton, *Stone* director John Curran was referencing Ingmar Bergman films and unabashedly talking about existentialism and the nature of spiritual revelation from the outset of the movie's production.[92] Still, *Stone* represents a rarity in the De Niro filmography in that the existential crisis of the character is largely articulated via sexuality, or a sexual dilemma. Soon enough, Mabry meets Stone's wife, Lucetta, who's initially seen as a very cheery and engaged kindergarten teacher. She's played by the lanky, beautiful Milla Jovavich, whose very strut speaks with a certain feral intensity. Lucetta believes that she can apply some of her own particularities of persuasion to her husband's case, and Mabry is initially very brusque and sincerely by-the-book in rebuffing her requests for a consultation.

But Mabry is weak, in ways he can't comprehend, let alone state. Alone in a field, he takes a golf swing and looks out at nothingness. Out of an impulse, he consults his church's pastor. "Sometimes the thoughts that I have, feelings … Sometimes I just think maybe you should shoot me …" The pastor, bland as room-temperature milk, says, "Well, I don't believe

that's what God wants for you." The frustrated Mabry asks, "What does he want?"

Soon after this, Lucetta tells Stone, "I've got him," and perhaps Mabry comes to believe that what God wants for him is the furtive ecstasy he experiences in his seduction by Lucetta, which she cheekily initiates by offering him an Easter egg crafted by her schoolkids. "I'm just eating the healthy part," Mabry tells her, trying to be charming. "Oh, go on, just eat the whole thing," the temptress responds.

The movie weaves its markers of spirituality—Easter eggs, talks of being "reborn," a subsequent religious epiphany experienced by Stone in the wake of his witnessing a prison murder (or does he? the incident passes without anything in the way of official recrimination, which suggests something odd afoot)—around the strong sexual component. And the film builds very deliberately from a face-off between two strong and strongly troubled characters, Mabry and Stone, into a three-way game once Lucetta enters the picture. In an unexpected move near the conclusion, Mabry's wife comes to the fore, like a previously unnoticed rook in a game of chess that suddenly leaps across the board to topple the king. The writing is complex, the directorial approach deceptively elliptical. For all its trappings of a genre thriller of character gamesmanship, for all its profane dialogue, the movie is ever extending into the mystic. After a discussion of Stone's crime, during

which Mabry can't help but reflect on the fact that he's having sex with the man's wife, Stone intuits Mabry's discomfort and advises him, "Just go ahead and burn your motherfuckin' life up … Just embrace it, man."

And Mabry does, but winds up embracing nothing. The film's coda places Mabry in a very uncomfortable purgatory, one of the features of which is the persistent buzzing of a wasp.

Digging In

While Norton had enjoyed working with De Niro on the 2002 heist picture *The Score*, which also featured Marlon Brando, making its cast a generational trifecta of uncanny, great performers, the experience was circumscribed by the movie's relative banality and the fact that the shoot was overseen by studio executives (see sidebar, page 165.) Actors always tell each other they'd like to work together, and sometimes they even mean it, but for Norton, a chance to work again with De Niro was devoutly wished for. In this case, during the initial stages of the film, there was every chance that it wouldn't happen. The movie had originated with director John Curran, who'd very much wanted to adapt Angus MacLachlan's play. Norton was not originally in the mix, although the actor's positive experience with the director on *The Painted Veil* (2006) left him eager to work with

De Niro with director John Curran on the set for the early scene where Mabry delivers a eulogy to his late brother.

Opposite: Scenes from Mabry's last official, preparole hearing interview with Stone.

Following pages: As his life unravels, Mabry sits on his veranda, whiskey and gun at hand, and thinks … what?

Curran again. De Niro, for his part, was also eager to have Norton on board.

"And finally by happenstance things dropped into place," Norton recalls. "And for me it was two things. As a filmmaker, I was excited to keep collaborating with John, and it was a chance to do something with Bob that I thought was really challenging. I thought the character, Stone, was actually sort of a little nerve-rackingly difficult. But I was really compelled by the idea of De Niro playing Jack, too. This is exactly the kind of thing that lazy people are always saying that Bob doesn't do anymore. It was dark and it was self-exposing and it was complex and it was kind of all the things I think that he is famous for."

As rehearsals began, a positive dynamic immediately established itself. Norton feels a lot of it had to do with Curran's approach, directing De Niro as a performer from whom he wants, and expects, a certain level of commitment and execution. "John's exactly the right kind of person, I think, for [De Niro] to work with. I think Bob loves directors like John personally, because, having worked with him in two different circumstances, I've seen that there are people who will fall into the trap of sort of venerating guys like Bob or Marlon. And when you do that, it automatically creates a distancing thing. I think it's like children who don't trust praise. I think Bob's way too sophisticated an artist to sit still for that. I think he's deeply

impatient with sort of the blather that comes with people not really working with you in a blunt and forceful way. People who don't really have the conviction of their own ideas, or have real ideas. And Curran is a very forceful thinker. He's very specific. He's very willing to try strange things. And he has no problem, with even as kind of a storied talent like Bob, just working right from the hip and asking a lot of him."

Norton's own search for his character led him to explore the prison where much of the movie would be shot, and there he found an inmate on whom he modeled Stone's look, swagger, mode of speech. "[H]is weird language and his verbiage and the way he talked, the stories he told, were so wild, I was just taping him. I had John come over to see if he liked it. And he loved it. So we almost just ripped, whole cloth, our old ideas of the character out"—the actors had rehearsed before heading for the locations— "and plugged in this other inspiration. And it was fun, because Bob hadn't seen that. I didn't have cornrows, and I didn't have that voice. John was really into the idea that when I kind of get pushed in front of him and we started shooting, it would be this thing he hadn't seen. And that's how we worked." This recalls the De Niro method of eliciting surprised reactions from fellow performers, one that Charles Grodin reversed on De Niro in *Midnight Run*; here the surprise is visual rather than verbal.

Stripping Down

"When we got up there in Detroit and did it," Norton recounts, "it was great. It was kind of quiet and intense, and there was no frills around it. I think we shot all the scenes between us in his office in, like, eight straight consecutive days. We didn't talk a lot between, we didn't go out for dinners. When we got done with it, I think for me and John it was exciting, because it was a real fulfillment of that fantasy of working with [De Niro] when he's really digging in on something and seeing him at work that way." A lot of the initial interaction between Mabry and Stone has Stone being voluble in a profane or raw metaphysical way, followed by Mabry's invariably constricted reactions. "One of his defining qualities is how intensely he listens," Norton observes. "He might be, like, one of the most powerful cinema actors ever *off the line*. I think he has what you can call the million-mile stare, but it's not just a stare. There's a deep sense with him, an ability to convey a very, very powerful, almost unnerving sense of an assessment that's going on inside him, of the situation that's taking place. And there's something about that which communicates a coiled internal pressure, or intensity, or whatever kind of bullshit reductive word you want to put on it."

Here Norton is articulating the thing that many critics have found so intriguing about

De Niro over the years; think of Andrew Sarris's observation about De Niro's ability to express suppressed, or barely suppressed, rage. While De Niro's skeptics bemoan the actor's lack of a certain versatility, believers (and the actors who work with him do tend to fall into this category) stand in awe of the purity of his expressive power, a power that often has nothing to do with the spoken word. "He's got this capacity to communicate this very, very powerful roiling inner life," Norton continues, "without a lot of words. He's sort of a Zen master to me because, he makes more out of silences than most people make out of pages of good writing. And he's tremendous at stripping things down to their essence. A lot of actors want more lines. But both times I've worked with him, he just takes a pen to the dialogue and kind of goes, 'I don't think I need to say that, I don't think I need to say that, I don't think I need to say that.' Almost to a fault."

Finding Lucetta

The intensity of the exchanges between the two actors, combined with their respective reputations, could lead one to minimize the contribution of Milla Jovovich. The part of Lucetta was originally to be played by an African-American actress. "[Curran] wanted her to be this black bombshell," Norton recalls. "I was into that idea, Bob was into that idea; we thought was great. John fought

It should have been great. As it stands, it isn't bad, particularly not when considered as the slightly-more-refined-than-average genre piece that it is, but one wanted, if not expected, more from *The Score*, directed by Frank Oz. The heist picture stars De Niro as an old-hand jewel thief tempted by the one-last-job lure; Edward Norton plays a young hotshot who wants to pull off something especially daring … and bringing the two together is a figure who's apparently even more venerated within the crime scene of Montreal, where the movie is set: a big lumbering fellow in a hat named Max, played by Marlon Brando. The scenes in which Norton, De Niro, and Brando interact have a peculiar energy to them. One of the main differences between Brando and De Niro as performers is that when the former is bored, he has all sorts of ways of letting you know it. With De Niro, however, even when the actor is turning in what a critic will disparage as a rote performance, the viewer doesn't see gears of personal dissatisfaction grinding underneath. Brando reportedly didn't care much for the material and enjoyed disparaging director Oz, citing his past with Jim Henson and the Muppets for special disapprobation. But as much as he smirks and wheezes, he also seems to enjoy the company of De Niro and Norton, and his delight as these two performers snipe at each other can be infectious.

The characters De Niro and Norton play are crooks, but throughout the movie they relate to each other as performers. "All you have to do is let the plot unfold," Cassandra Wilson, the jazz singer, coos in a song in one scene set in the nightclub De Niro's character runs. And all of the thrusting and parrying between the three characters has to do with how the plot will unfold, and who's going to play the lead. During the heist itself, Norton asks De Niro at one point, "Are you there?" and De Niro responds "I'm on my mark."

"The thing that seemed fun about it to me," Norton recalls, "was the notion of people who were at different phases of a career and a life and the way that you're going to end up. An observation on the idea of character is destiny. There were some fun analogous character streaks that one could project onto me, and Bob, and Marlon respectively, that sort of overlaid in a nice way."[g] The film would turn out to be Brando's last. "I did it because of the two of them, needless to say."[h]

a really, really hard fight with the financiers of the film over that." As Norton explains, foreign sales packages often buttress a movie's financing, especially so when it comes to an ambitious project like this one; the demand was for a name. Milla Jovavich, as it happens, is marketable because of her work in the highly successful sci-fi/horror/video game-spinoff franchise *Resident Evil*. Norton thought she would be a good fit for a different reason. "I had met her years ago, on an audition, and I had been really struck by how kind of authentically of the street she was. And of course she's in Spike Lee's *He Got Game* [1998], which I told John to check out."

While Mabry is struggling with the revelation that the value system he believes he's tried to honor his entire life now appears to him as a lie if not a bad joke and Stone struggles in his way toward a kind of redemption or at least spiritual instrumentality, Lucetta, as Norton puts it, "doesn't have moral quandaries. She's an animal. She's still in the animal phase. She's not immoral; she's genuinely amoral. I think Milla's own guilelessness made that work. And I think she made Bob really uncomfortable."

"A Genuinely Challenging, Difficult Movie"

Despite its mixed reception critically and the fact that it came and went from theaters practically unnoticed, *Stone* is a major De Niro performance in what's possibly a major film. Like much of De Niro's work with Scorsese, it contains unresolved intimations that nip at the viewer's psychic heels in ways that more conventional stories don't. "*Taxi Driver* isn't the movie that a lot of people think it is, or like to remember it as. It's a genuinely challenging, difficult movie," Norton observed during our discussion. "Those movies that De Niro and Scorsese made, they make you so uncomfortable and they pick up under the skin of so many of the things that people don't want to look at. You take *Taxi Driver* for granted because now it's de rigueur for like films to try to get into dysfunctional characters, things like that. And I think now we take it for granted that you can make those kinds of movies. But when you think about the balls [it took] to make that movie at that time, you just have to not give a fuck, you know what I mean?"

Conclusion

At the end of April 2013, *The Big Wedding* opened across the United States. The movie chronicles the frantic attempts of an affluent and highly dysfunctional American family to put on a show of unity for the sake of strait-laced relatives flying in from overseas for the title event. De Niro plays the rakish patriarch of the American brood; Diane Keaton, who played Kay Corleone in the fifties scenes of *The Godfather Part II*, plays De Niro's ex-wife; Susan Sarandon is De Niro's "feisty" current love interest; Robin Williams, De Niro's costar in *Awakenings*, plays a priest; Topher Grace, Amanda Seyfried, Katherine Heigl, and Ben Barnes are the young people of the cast.

De Niro's role is of the sort that, in the early part of his career, he seemed to have no interest in playing: that of a relatively contented bourgeois. And he does a better-than-serviceable job of it; while *The Big Wedding* is nobody's idea of a good movie, the actors bring a lot more to it than the material demands or deserves. Keaton and De Niro are particularly good and occasionally very funny together. Almost simultaneous with the opening of *The Big Wedding*, New York's Tribeca Film Festival, De Niro's brainchild, hosted the premiere of a restoration of *The King of Comedy*. Watching this supremely uncomfortable film with the subway-poster image of the aged, natty De Niro chortling in deliberately overplayed fake joviality in the ads for *The Big Wedding* held in the back of one's mind could result in a moment of supreme cognitive dissonance for a movie lover.

Does *The Big Wedding* make *The King of Comedy* less coruscating, less "true"? I suppose that's up to the individual viewer. There's still a vivid sense in the culture of De Niro as a yardstick, if not for a certain brand of gravitas, then for a standard of competence, or super-competence. In 2013 he received an Academy Award nomination in the Best Supporting Actor category for his work in the film *Silver Linings Playbook*. The film, directed by David O. Russell, gave De Niro a meaty role. Still, the larger function of De Niro's work in the movie was to reflect well on the younger leads in the cast; part of the buzz pertaining to female lead Jennifer Lawrence, for instance, had to do with how she "held her own" opposite De Niro. On the cover of the April 2013 issue of the UK edition of *GQ*, *SLP* lead Bradley Cooper is the star; "It's Time to Take Bradley Cooper Seriously," says the main cover line, and below it, in smaller type: "(Don't take our word for it: ask Robert De Niro.)"

De Niro, aged seventy at the publication of this book, continues to make films at a breakneck pace. In a recent interview he explained why: "Time is precious. I have to do all these movies I want to do. I can't really put them off for two years. I have this movie that I've been wanting to do with Scorsese, and we set a date to start shooting in two years. But we're talking about time. I mean, you want to be able to stand up when you do a movie."[93] The reporter then asked De Niro about *New Year's Eve* (2011), a frankly awful multi-storyline romantic comedy. "I do make choices that are whatever, but I … it is what it is. It paid well and I found myself in a situation where I had to weigh whether to do this or to do that, and I like [director] Garry Marshall. It is what it is."[94]

In 1975, reporting from the set of *Taxi Driver*, the journalist taglined "N.C." wrote: "Five or six years ago, De Niro started writing a screenplay. It concerned an assassination-obsessed young man (as does *Taxi Driver*) who dreamed of taking a gun, going to the United Nations, and killing a famous person. The script never got finished but was obviously on De Niro's mind when he read Schrader's *Taxi Driver*. 'One time before we all kind of hit it big, I was discussing Bobby's script with him,' says Schrader. 'I said to him, "Do you know what the gun in your script represents?" I said it was obvious to me that it was his talent, which was like a loaded gun hidden in him that nobody would let him shoot, and that if somebody would just let him fire once, the whole world would see the enormous impact his talent would have.'"[95]

"Bang," "N.C." concludes the account. And Schrader was right: the impact was enormous. And we viewers and critics can't really tell what the recoil was like. And, at the risk of overplaying this metaphor, the question of De Niro's remaining ammunition can be answered only film by film.

Following pages: De Niro as Neil McCauley in *Heat* (1995), directed by Michael Mann.

1943
Robert De Niro Jr., child of Robert De Niro and Virginia Admiral, is born on August 17 in New York City. The then-married parents would separate shortly thereafter, but their divorce was not made final until 1957.

1953
De Niro, aged ten, makes his first stage appearance at Maria Ley-Piscator's dramatic workshop, in the role of the Cowardly Lion in a production of *The Wizard of Oz*.

1959
Teenage De Niro travels to Europe, first to visit his father, living in Paris at the time. Hitches around the Continent for several months.

1960–1963
Having dropped out of high school, De Niro audits classes at Stella Adler's Conservatory of Actors.

1963
Successfully auditions for, and acts in, a supporting role in *The Wedding Party*, a low-budget film being made by Sarah Lawrence professor Wilford Leach and two students, Brian De Palma and Cynthia Munroe. The film is not released until 1969.

1965
Acts in the never-released film *Encounter*, costarring with Dyanne Thorne, who ten years later would achieve grindhouse notoriety as "Ilsa, She Wolf of the SS."

Has a small role in French master Marcel Carné's New York–shot *Three Rooms in Manhattan*.

1967–1968
Appears in a touring rep production of *Tchin-Tchin* by Sidney Michaels.
Plays all ten male roles in the play *Glamour, Glory and Gold*, starring drag performers Holly Woodlawn and Candy Darling.
Meets actresses Sally Kirkland and Shelley Winters.
Acquires his first agent, Richard Bauman.
Greetings, his first film with Brian De Palma as sole director, opens in December of 1968.

1969
Shoots *Bloody Mama*, starring his friend and mentor Shelley Winters, in Arkansas, with "King of the Bs" Roger Corman directing. Bruce Dern and Robert Walden are among his costars.

1971
Plays a police officer for the first time in a film, an undercover narcotics operative who tries to get junkie George Segal to pull off a scam, in *Born to Win*, Czech director Ivan Passer's first US film.

1972
Is formally introduced to director Martin Scorsese by Brian De Palma at a Christmas party hosted by critic and screenwriter Jay Cocks and his wife, the actress Verna Bloom.

1973
Shoots *Mean Streets* under Scorsese's direction, playing the role of Johnny Boy.

1974
Finishes shooting *The Godfather Part II* with Francis Ford Coppola.
Commences *Novocento* with director Bernardo Bertolucci, costarring with Gerard Depardieu, in Parma, Italy.

1975
Wins Best Supporting Actor Academy Award for playing Vito Corleone in *The Godfather Part II*.

1976
Marries actress Diahnne Abbott and adopts her daughter from a prior relationship, Dreena.
Taxi Driver released.

1977
De Niro and Abbott's son, Raphael, is born in January. De Niro receives a Best Actor Oscar nomination for his work in *Taxi Driver*.

1979
De Niro and Abbott agree to separate. They will not finalize their divorce until 1988. Receives Best Actor Academy Award nomination for his work in Michael Cimino's *The Deer Hunter*.

1981
Wins Best Actor Academy Award for *Raging Bull*, in a ceremony that has been postponed for a day after John Hinckley's attempt to assassinate President Ronald Reagan.

1984
Attends the Cannes Film Festival in May to promote *Once Upon a Time in America*, the unstuck-in-time Sergio Leone gangster epic in which he plays "Noodles" Aaronson. The four-hour film will be severely mutilated for its initial US release.

1985
Plays his first supporting role since the early seventies: the anarchist plumber Harry Tuttle, in Terry Gilliam's dystopian fantasy *Brazil*, a legendarily fraught production.

1986
Returns to live theater for producer Joseph Papp in Reinaldo Povod's *Cuba and His Teddy Bear*. It is De Niro's first, and thus far only, engagement in Broadway theater.

1987
Serves as President of the Jury at the 15th Moscow International Film Festival.

1989
De Niro, with real estate developer Paul Wallace and impresario Stuart Lane, buys the former Martinson Coffee Building in lower Manhattan, at the intersection of Greenwich and Franklin. Work begins on what will become the Tribeca Center, featuring the restaurant Tribeca Bar and Grill and holding the offices of De Niro's production company Tribeca Film.

Reunites with director Martin Scorsese for the gangster film *Goodfellas*.

1991
De Niro receives a Lifetime Achievement Award from the American Museum of the Moving Image.
Receives Best Actor Academy Award nomination for his work in *Awakenings*.

1992
De Niro receives a Best Actor Academy Award nomination for his work in the Martin Scorsese–directed *Cape Fear*.

1993
In partnership with chef Nobuyuki Matsuhisa, opens a New York branch of the Japanese restaurant Nobu in Tribeca.

1995
Fathers twin boys, Julian Henry and Aaron Kendrick. Their mother is model Toukie Smith; the children were conceived through in vitro fertilization and carried and delivered by a surrogate.

1997
Marries his second wife, Grace Hightower.
His increased work pace is reflected in the fact that three films in which he plays major roles, *Cop Land*, *Jackie Brown*, and *Wag the Dog* are released in the US between the months of August and December.

1998
Son Elliott is born to De Niro and Grace Hightower.

2002
Inaugurates Tribeca Film Festival with Tribeca Film partner Jane Rosenthal and her husband, real estate investor Craig Hatkoff.

2003
Is diagnosed with prostate cancer. Undergoes successful treatment.

2004
De Niro and Grace Hightower, who did not finalize their 2001 divorce, renew their marriage vows.

2006
Is conferred honorary Italian citizenship at the Rome Film Festival.
His second feature film as director, *The Good Shepherd*, premieres.

2008
Appears at a rally supporting presidential candidate Barack Obama at New Jersey's Izod Center.

2011
Is awarded the Cecil B. DeMille Honors Lifetime Achievement Award by the Hollywood Foreign Press Association at the Golden Globes Awards.
De Niro and Grace Hightower have their second child, daughter Helen Grace.

2013
Receives Best Supporting Actor Academy Award nomination for his work in *Silver Linings Playbook*.
In September, announces that he will take the role on the HBO miniseries *Criminal Justice* that had originally been that of James Gandolfini, the *Sopranos* actor who died in June 2013.

Page 172: De Niro in Bernardo Bertolucci's *1900* (1976), Martin Scorsese's *New York, New York* (1977), Michael Cimino's *The Deer Hunter* (1978), and Ulu Grosbard's *True Confessions* (1981).

Opposite: ... and in Sergio Leone's *Once Upon a Time in America* (1984), Martin Scorsese's *Cape Fear* (1991), Joel Schumacher's *Flawless* (1999), and Ethan Maniquis and Robert Rodriguez's *Machete* (2010).

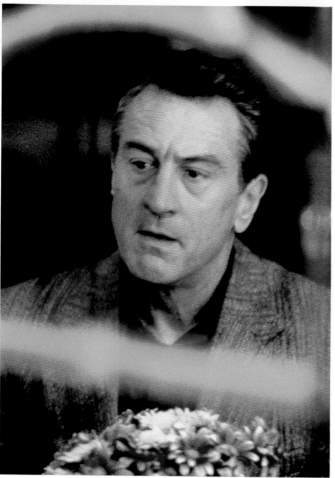

1965

Trois chambres à Manhattan (Three Rooms in Manhattan)
Directed by Marcel Carné *Screenplay* Marcel Carné, Jacques Sigurd, from a novel by Georges Simenon *Cinematography* Eugen Shüfftan *Set Decoration* Léon Barsacq, Mayo, Gabriel Béchir *Original Music* Martial Solal, Mal Waldron *Film Editing* Henri Rust *Produced by* Charles Lumbroso. With Annie Girardot (Kay Larsi), Maurice Ronet (François Combe), O. E. Hasse (Hourvitch). De Niro has an uncredited bit role as a diner patron.

1968

Greetings
Directed by Brian De Palma *Screenplay* Brian De Palma, Charles Hirsch *Cinematography* Robert Fiore *Original Music* Eric Kaz, Stephen Soles, Artie Traum *Film Editing* Brian De Palma *Produced by* Charles Hirsch. With Gerrit Graham (Lloyd Clay), Robert De Niro (Jon Rubin), Jonathan Warden (Paul Shaw), Rutanya Alda (Linda).

1969

The Wedding Party
Directed by Brian De Palma, Wilford Leach, Cynthia Munroe *Screenplay* Brian De Palma, Wilford Leach, Cynthia Munroe *Cinematography* Peter Powell *Original Music* John Herbert McDowell *Film Editing* Brian De Palma, Wilford Leach, Cynthia Munroe *Produced by* Brian De Palma, Wilford Leach, Cynthia Munroe. With Charles Pfluger (Charlie), William Finley (Alistair), Robert De Niro (Cecil) (as "Robert Denero"), Jill Clayburgh (Josephine), Richard Kolmar (Jean-Claude/Singh/Klaus), Jennifer Salt (Phoebe).

Sam's Song
Directed by Jordan Leondopoulos *Screenplay* Jordan Leondopoulos *Cinematography* Álex Phillips Jr. *Original Music* Gershon Kingsley *Film Editing* Arline Garson *Produced by* Christopher C. Dewey. With Robert De Niro (Sam Nicoletti), Jennifer Warren (Erica Moore), Jarred Mickey (Andrew Moore).

1970

Bloody Mama
Directed by Roger Corman *Screenplay* Don Peters, Robert Thom *Cinematography* John Alonzo *Set Decoration* Michael Ross *Original Music* Don Randi *Film Editing* Eve Newman *Produced by* Samuel Z. Arkoff, Roger Corman, Norman T. Herman, James H. Nicholson. With Shelley Winters ("Ma" Kate Barker), Bruce Dern (Kevin Dirkman), Don Stroud (Herman Barker), Clint Kimbrough (Arthur Barker) Alex Nicol (George Barker), Robert Walden (Fred Barker) Robert De Niro (Lloyd Barker), Diane Varsi (Mona Gibson), Pat Hingle (Sam Adams Pendlebury), Scatman Crothers (Moses).

Hi, Mom!
Directed by Brian De Palma *Screenplay* Brian De Palma *Cinematography* Robert Elfstrom *Set Decoration* Pete Bocour *Original Music* Eric Kaz *Film Editing* Paul Hirsch *Produced by* Charles Hirsch. With Robert De Niro (Jon Rubin), Charles Durning (Superintendent), Allen Garfield (Joe Banner), Gerrit Graham (Gerrit Wood), Jennifer Salt (Judy Bishop), Paul Bartel (Uncle Tom Wood).

1971

Jennifer on My Mind
Directed by Noel Black *Screenplay* Erich Segal, from the novel by Roger L. Simon *Cinematography* Andrew Laszlo *Set Decoration* Alan Hicks *Original Music* Stephen Lawrence *Film Editing* Jack Wheeler *Produced by* Bernard Schwartz, Philip Hazelton. With Michael Brandon (Marcus), Tippy Walker (Jenny), Peter Bonerz (Sergei), Renée Taylor (Selma), Robert De Niro (Mardigian), Barry Bostwick (Nanki,) Jeff Conaway (Hanki).

Born to Win
Directed by Ivan Passer *Screenplay* David Scott Milton, Ivan Passer *Cinematography* Jack Priestley, Richard Kratina *Set Decoration* Murray P. Stern *Original Music* William S. Fischer *Film Editing* Ralph Rosenbaum *Produced by* Philip Langner, Jerry Tokofsky. With George Segal (J), Karen Black (Parm), Paula Prentiss (Veronica), Hector Elizondo (Vivian), Robert De Niro (Danny).

The Gang That Couldn't Shoot Straight
Directed by James Goldstone *Screenplay* Waldo Salt, from the novel by Jimmy Breslin *Cinematography* Owen Roizman *Set Decoration* George DeTitta Sr *Original Music* Dave Grusin *Film Editing* Edward A. Biery *Produced by* Robert Chartoff, Irwin Winkler. With Jerry Orbach (Kid Sally), Leigh Taylor-Young (Angela), Jo Van Fleet (Big Momma), Lionel Stander (Baccala), Robert De Niro (Mario), Hervé Villechaize (Beppo), Burt Young (Willie Quarequlo), Margo Winkler (Airline Clerk), Michael V. Gazzo (A Black Suit).

1973

Bang the Drum Slowly
Directed by John Hancock *Screenplay* Mark Harris, from his novel *Cinematography* Richard Shore *Set Decoration* Frederic C. Weiler *Original Music* Stephen Lawrence *Film Editing* Richard Marks *Produced by* Lois Rosenfield and Maurice Rosenfield. With Michael Moriarty (Henry "Author" Wiggen), Robert De Niro (Bruce Pearson), Vincent Gardenia (Dutch Schnell), Barbara Babcock (Team Owner), Marshall Efron (Bradley), Danny Aiello (Horse).

Mean Streets
Directed by Martin Scorsese *Screenplay* Martin Scorsese, Mardik Martin *Cinematography* Kent Wakeford *Set Decoration* Bill Bates *Film Editing* Sidney Levin *Produced by* Jonathan T. Taplin, E. Lee Perry. With Harvey Keitel (Charlie), Robert De Niro (Johnny Boy),

David Proval (Tony), Richard Romanus (Michael), Amy Robinson (Teresa), Cesare Danova (Giovanni), George Memmoli (Joey), David Carradine (Drunk), Robert Carradine (Boy with Gun), Harry Northrup (Soldier), Martin Scorsese (Shorty).

1974
The Godfather Part II
Directed by Francis Ford Coppola *Screenplay* Francis Ford Coppola, Mario Puzo. *Cinematography* Gordon Willis *Set Decoration* George R. Nelson, under supervision of Dean Tavoularis, production designer *Original Music* Nino Rota *Film Editing* Barry Malkin, Richard Marks, Peter Zinner *Produced by* Francis Ford Coppola, Gray Frederickson, Fred Roos. With Al Pacino (Michael Corleone), Diane Keaton (Kay Corleone), John Cazale (Fredo Corleone) Robert De Niro (Vito Corleone), Robert Duvall (Tom Hagen), Lee Strasberg (Hyman Roth), Danny Aiello (Tony Rosato), Joe Spinell (Willi Cicci), Dominic Chianese (Johnny Ola), Bruno Kirby (Clemenza), Michael V. Gazzo (Frankie Pentangeli), G. D. Spradlin (Senator Pat Geary), Richard Bright (Al Neri).

1976
Taxi Driver
Directed by Martin Scorsese *Screenplay* Paul Schrader *Cinematography* Michael Chapman *Set Decoration* Herbert F. Mulligan *Original Music* Bernard Herrmann *Film Editing* Tom Rolf, Melvin Shapiro *Produced by* Michael Phillips, Julia Phillips. With Robert De Niro (Travis Bickle), Jodie Foster (Iris), Harvey Keitel (Sport), Peter Boyle (Wizard), Harry Northup (Doughboy), Leonard Harris (Charles Palantine), Cybill Shepherd (Betsy), Albert Brooks (Tom), Diahnne Abbott (Concession Girl), Gene Palma (Street Drummer), Murray

Moston (Iris's Timekeeper) Steven Prince (Andy), Peter Savage (The John), Martin Scorsese (Passenger Watching Silhouette).

1900
Directed by Bernardo Bertolucci *Screenplay* Bernardo Bertolucci, Franco Arcalli, Giuseppe Bertolucci *Cinematography* Vittorio Storaro *Set Decoration* Maria Paola Maino *Original Music* Ennio Morricone *Film Editing* Franco Arcalli *Produced by* Alberto Grimaldi. With Gerard Depardieu (Olmo Dalcò), Robert De Niro (Alfredo Berlinghieri), Dominique Sanda (Ada Fiastri Paulhan), Laura Betti (Regina), Stefania Casini (Neve), Sterling Hayden (Leo Dalcò), Donald Sutherland (Attila Mellanchini), Burt Lancaster (Alfredo Berlinghieri the Elder).

The Last Tycoon
Directed by Elia Kazan *Screenplay* Harold Pinter, from the novel by F. Scott Fitzgerald *Cinematography* Victor J. Kemper *Set Decoration* Jerry Wunderlich *Original Music* Maurice Jarre *Film Editing* Richard Marks *Produced by* Sam Spiegel. With Robert De Niro (Monroe Stahr), Teresa Russell (Cecilia Brady), Ingrid Boulting (Kathleen Moore), Robert Mitchum (Pat Brady), Jeanne Moreau (Didi), Ray Milland (Fleishacker), Dana Andrews (Red Ridingwood), Donald Pleasence (Boxley), Jack Nicholson (Brimmer), John Carradine (Tour Guide), Anjelica Huston (Edna).

1977
New York, New York
Directed by Martin Scorsese *Screenplay* Earl Mac Rauch, Mardik Martin *Cinematography* László Kovács *Set Decoration* Robert De Vestel, Ruby R. Levitt, under supervision of Boris Leven, production designer *Original Music* John Kander,

Fred Ebb *Film Editing* Bert Lovitt, David Ramirez, Tom Rolf *Produced by* Robert Chartoff, Irwin Winkler. With Liza Minnelli (Francine Evans), Robert De Niro (Jimmy Doyle), Lionel Stander (Tony Harwell), Barry Primus (Paul Wilson), Dick Miller (Palm Club Owner), Murray Moston (Horace Morris).

1978
The Deer Hunter
Directed by Michael Cimino *Screenplay* Deric Washburn *Cinematography* Vilmos Zsigmond *Set Decoration* Richard C. Goddard, Alan Hicks *Original Music* Stanley Myers *Film Editing* Peter Zinner *Produced by* Michael Cimino, Michael Deeley, John Peverall, Barry Spikings. With Robert De Niro (Michael), Christopher Walken (Nick), John Savage (Steven), John Cazale (Stan), Meryl Streep (Linda), George Dzundza (John), Rutanya Alda (Angela).

1980
Raging Bull
Directed by Martin Scorsese *Screenplay* Paul Schrader, Mardik Martin *Cinematography* Michael Chapman *Set Decoration* Phil Abramson, Frederic C. Weiler, Carl Biddiscombe *Film Editing* Thelma Schoonmaker *Produced by* Robert Chartoff, Irwin Winkler. With Robert De Niro (Jake La Motta), Joe Pesci (Joey), Cathy Moriarty (Vickie La Motta), Frank Vincent (Salvy), Nicholas Colasanto (Tommy Como), Teresa Saldana (Lenore), Lori Ann Flax (Irma), Martin Scorsese (Barbizon Stagehand).

1981
True Confessions
Directed by Ulu Grosbard *Screenplay* John Gregory Dunne, Joan Didion, from the novel by Dunne *Cinematography* Owen Roizman *Set Decoration* Marvin March *Original Music* Georges Delerue *Film*

Editing Lynzee Klingman *Produced by* Robert Chartoff, Irwin Winkler. With Robert Duvall (Det. Tom Spellacy), Robert De Niro (Father Des Spellacy), Charles Durning (Jack Amsterdam), Kenneth McMillan (Frank Crotty), Cyril Cusack (Cardinal Danaher), Burgess Meredith (Msgr. Seamus Fargo), Jeanette Nolan (Mrs. Spellacy).

1983
The King of Comedy
Directed by Martin Scorsese *Screenplay* Paul D. Zimmerman *Cinematography* Fred Schuler *Set Decoration* George DeTitta Sr., Daniel Robert, under supervision of Boris Leven, Production Design *Film Editing* Thelma Schoonmaker *Produced by* Arnon Milchan. With Robert De Niro (Rupert Pupkin), Jerry Lewis (Jerry Langford), Sandra Bernhard (Masha), Diahnne Abbott (Rita), Shelley Hack (Cathy Long), Fred De Cordova (Bert Thomas), Martin Scorsese (TV Director), Tony Randall, Dr. Joyce Brothers, Ed Herlihy, Lou Brown (themselves).

1984
Once Upon a Time in America
Directed by Sergio Leone *Screenplay* Sergio Leone, Franco Arcalli, Leonardo Benvenuti, Piero De Bernardi, Franco Ferrini, Enrico Medioli, from a novel by Harry Grey *Cinematography* Tonino Delli Colli *Set Decoration* Bruno Cesari, Osvaldo Desideri *Original Music* Ennio Morricone *Film Editing* Nino Baragli *Produced by* Arnon Milchan. With James Woods (Maximilian Bercovicz), Robert De Niro (David "Noodles" Aaronson), Elizabeth McGovern (Deborah Gelly), Burt Young (Joe), Tuesday Weld (Carol), Treat Williams (James Conway O'Donnell), Danny Aiello (Police Chief Vincent Aiello), Darlanne Fluegel (Eve), William Forsythe (Philip

"Cockeye" Stein), Richard Bright (Chicken Joe), James Russo (Bugsy).

Falling in Love
Directed by Ulu Grosbard *Screenplay* Michael Cristofer *Cinematography* Peter Suschitzky *Set Decoration* Steven J. Jordan *Original Music* Dave Grusin *Film Editing* Michael Kahn *Produced by* Marvin Worth. With Meryl Streep (Molly Gilmore), Robert De Niro (Frank Raftis), Harvey Keitel (Ed Lasky), Jane Kaczmarek (Ann Raftis), George Martin (John Trainer), David Clennon (Brian Gilmore).

1985
Brazil
Directed by Terry Gilliam *Screenplay* Terry Gilliam, Tom Stoppard, Charles McKeown *Cinematography* Roger Pratt *Original Music* Michael Kamen *Film Editing* Julian Doyle *Produced by* Arnon Milchan. With Jonathan Pryce (Sam Lowry), Kim Greist (Jill Layton), Robert De Niro (Harry Tuttle), Ian Holm (Mr. Kurtzmann), Bob Hoskins (Spoor), Michael Palin (Jack Lint), Jim Broadbent (Dr. Jaffe), Katherine Helmond (Mrs. Ida Lowry).

1986
The Mission
Directed by Roland Joffé *Screenplay* Robert Bolt *Cinematography* Chris Menges *Original Music* Ennio Morricone *Film Editing* Jim Clark *Produced by* David Puttnam, Fernando Ghia. With Robert De Niro (Rodrigo Mendoza), Jeremy Irons (Father Gabriel), Aidan Quinn (Felipe Mendoza), Liam Neeson (Fielding).

1987
Angel Heart
Directed by Alan Parker *Screenplay* Alan Parker, from a novel by William Hjortsberg *Cinematography* Michael Seresin *Set Decoration*

Robert J. Franco, Leslie Pope *Original Music* Trevor Jones *Film Editing* Gerry Hambling *Produced by* Elliott Kastner, Alan Marshall. With Mickey Rourke (Harry Angel), Robert De Niro (Louis Cyphre), Lisa Bonet (Epiphany Proudfoot), Charlotte Rampling (Margaret Krusemark), Brownie McGhee (Toots Sweet), Dann Florek (Herman Winesap).

The Untouchables
Directed by Brian De Palma *Screenplay* David Mamet *Cinematography* Stephen H. Burum *Set Decoration* Hal Gausman *Original Music* Ennio Morricone *Film Editing* Jerry Greenberg, Bill Pankow *Produced by* Art Linson. With Kevin Costner (Eliot Ness), Sean Connery (Jim Malone), Charles Martin Smith (Agent Oscar Wallace), Andy Garcia (Agent George Stone/Giuseppe Petri), Robert De Niro (Al Capone), Billy Drago (Frank Nitti), Patricia Clarkson (Catherine Ness.)

1988
Midnight Run
Directed by Martin Brest *Screenplay* George Gallo *Cinematography* Donald Thorin *Set Decoration* George R. Nelson *Original Music* Danny Elfman *Film Editing* Chris Lebenzon, Michael Tronick, Billy Weber *Produced by* Martin Brest. With Robert De Niro (Jack Walsh), Charles Grodin (Jonathan Mardukas), Yaphet Kotto (Alonzo Mosely), John Ashton (Marvin Dorfler), Dennis Farina (Jimmy Serrano), Joe Pantoliano (Eddie Moscone), Wendy Phillips (Gail), Philip Baker Hall (Sidney).

1989
Jacknife
Directed by David Hugh Jones *Screenplay* Stephen Metcalfe, from his stage play. *Cinematography* Brian West *Set Decoration* Gilles Aird, Robert J. Franco *Original Music* Bruce Broughton

Film Editing John Bloom *Produced by* Carol Baum, Robert Schaffel. With Robert De Niro (Joseph "Jacknife" Megessey), Kathy Baker (Martha Flannigan), Ed Harris (David "High School" Flannigan), Charles S. Dutton (Jake), Loudon Wainwright III (Ferretti), George Gerdes (Tony), Josh Pais (Rick).

We're No Angels
Directed by Neil Jordan *Screenplay* David Mamet, suggested by Ranald MacDougall *Cinematography* Philippe Rousselot *Set Decoration* Jim Erickson *Original Music* George Fenton *Film Editing* Mick Audsley, Joke van Wijk *Produced by* Art Linson. With Robert De Niro (Ned), Sean Penn (Jim), Demi Moore (Molly), Hoyt Axton (Father Levesque), Bruno Kirby (Deputy), James Russo (Bobby), Wallace Shawn (Translator), John C. Reilly (Young Monk).

1990
Stanley and Iris
Directed by Martin Ritt *Screenplay* Harriet Frank Jr., Irving Ravetch, from a novel by Pat Barker *Cinematography* Donald McAlpine *Set Decoration* Les Bloom, Steve Shewchuk *Original Music* John Williams *Film Editing* Sidney Levin *Produced by* Arlene Sellers, Alex Winitsky. With Robert De Niro (Stanley Cox), Jane Fonda (Iris King), Swoosie Kurtz (Sharon), Martha Plimpton (Kelly), Jamey Sheridan (Joe), Feodor Chaliapin Jr. (Leonides Cox), Zohra Lampert (Elaine).

Goodfellas
Directed by Martin Scorsese *Screenplay* Martin Scorsese, Nicholas Pileggi, from Pileggi's book *Wise Guy* *Cinematography* Michael Ballhaus *Set Decoration* Les Bloom *Film Editing* James Y. Kwei, Thelma Schoonmaker *Produced by* Irwin Winkler. With Ray Liotta (Henry

Hill), Robert De Niro (James Conway), Joe Pesci (Tommy DeVito), Paul Sorvino (Paul Cicero), Frank Vincent (Billy Batts), Chuck Low (Morris Kessler), Lorraine Bracco (Karen Hill).

Awakenings
Directed by Penny Marshall *Screenplay* Steven Zaillian, from a book by Oliver Sacks *Cinematography* Miroslav Ondříček *Set Decoration* George DeTitta Jr. *Original Music* Randy Newman *Film Editing* Battle Davis, Jerry Greenberg *Produced by* Walter F. Parkes, Lawrence Lasker. With Robin Williams (Dr. Malcolm Sayer), Robert De Niro (Leonard Lowe), Ruth Nelson (Mrs. Lowe), Penelope Ann Miller (Paula), Judith Malina (Rose), Anne Meara (Miriam), John Heard (Dr. Kaufman), Julie Kavner (Eleanor Costello), Dexter Gordon (Rolando).

1991
Guilty By Suspicion
Directed by Irwin Winkler *Screenplay* Irwin Winkler *Cinematography* Michael Ballhaus *Set Decoration* Nancy Haigh *Original Music* James Newton Howard *Film Editing* Priscilla Nedd *Produced by* Arnon Milchan. With Robert De Niro (David Merrill), Annette Bening (Ruth Merrill), George Wendt (Bunny Baxter), Sam Wanamaker (Felix Graff), Chris Cooper (Larry Nolan), Martin Scorsese (Joseph Lesser), Barry Primus (Bert Alan), Ben Piazza (Daryl Zanuck).

Backdraft
Directed by Ron Howard *Screenplay* Gregory Widen *Cinematography* Mikael Salomon *Set Decoration* Garrett Lewis *Original Music* Hans Zimmer *Film Editing* Daniel Hanley, Michael Hill *Produced by* Pen Densham, Larry DeWaay, Richard B. Lewis, John Watson. With Kurt Russell (Stephen "Bull"

McCaffrey), William Baldwin (Brian McCaffrey), Robert De Niro (Donald "Shadow" Rimgale), Donald Sutherland (Ronald Bartel), Jennifer Jason Leigh (Jennifer Vaitkus), Scott Glenn (John "Axe" Adcox), Rebecca De Mornay (Helen McCaffrey), J. T. Walsh (Alderman Marty Swayzak).

Cape Fear

Directed by Martin Scorsese *Screenplay* Wesley Strick, from a novel by John D. MacDonald and a screenplay by James R. Webb *Cinematography* Freddie Francis *Set Decoration* Alan Hicks *Film Editing* Thelma Schoonmaker *Produced by* Barbara De Fina. With Robert De Niro (Max Cady), Nick Nolte (Sam Bowden), Jessica Lange (Leigh Bowden), Juliette Lewis (Danielle Bowden), Joe Don Baker (Claude Kersek), Robert Mitchum (Lieutenant Elgart), Gregory Peck (Lee Heller), Martin Balsam (Judge), Illeana Douglas (Lori Davis).

1992
Mistress

Directed by Barry Primus *Screenplay* Barry Primus, J. F. Lawton *Cinematography* Sven Kirsten *Set Decoration* K. C. Fox *Original Music* Galt MacDermot *Film Editing* Steven Weisberg *Produced by* Meir Teper, Robert De Niro. With Robert Wuhl (Marvin Landisman), Martin Landau (Jack Roth), Eli Wallach (George Lieberhof), Danny Aiello (Carmine Rasso), Jean Smart (Patricia Riley) Robert De Niro (Evan M. Wright).

Night and the City

Directed by Irwin Winkler *Screenplay* Richard Price, from the novel by Gerald Kersh *Cinematography* Tak Fujimoto *Set Decoration* Robert J. Franco *Original Music* James Newton Howard *Film Editing* David Brenner *Produced by* Irwin Winkler, Jane Rosenthal. With Robert De Niro (Harry Fabian), Jessica Lange (Helen Nasseros), Cliff Gorman (Phil

Nasseros), Alan King (Ira "Boom Boom" Grossman), Jack Warden (Al Grossman), Eli Wallach (Peck), Barry Primus (Tommy Tessler).

1993
Mad Dog and Glory

Directed by John McNaughton *Screenplay* Richard Price *Cinematography* Robby Müller *Set Decoration* Leslie Pope *Original Music* Elmer Bernstein, Terphe Rypdal *Film Editing* Elena Maganini, Craig McKay *Produced by* Martin Scorsese, Barbara De Fina. With Robert De Niro (Wayne "Mad Dog" Dobie), Uma Thurman (Glory), Bill Murray (Frank Milo), Kathy Baker (Lee), David Caruso (Mike).

This Boy's Life

Directed by Michael Caton-Jones *Screenplay* Robert Getchell, from the book by Tobias Wolff *Cinematography* David Watkin *Set Decoration* Jim Erickson *Original Music* Carter Burwell *Film Editing* Jim Clark *Produced by* Art Linson, Fitch Cady. With Robert De Niro (Dwight), Ellen Barkin (Caroline), Leonardo DiCaprio (Toby), Chris Cooper (Roy), Carla Gugino (Norma), Tobey Maguire (Chuck Bolger).

A Bronx Tale

Directed by Robert De Niro *Screenplay* Chazz Palminteri, from his play *Cinematography* Reynaldo Villalobos *Set Decoration* Debra Schutt *Original Music* Butch Barbella *Film Editing* R. Q. Lovett, David Ray *Produced by* Robert De Niro, Jon Kilik, Jane Rosenthal. With Robert De Niro (Lorenzo Anello), Chazz Palminteri (Sonny LoSpecchio), Lillo Brancato (Calogero "C" Anello), Joe Pesci (Carmine), Kathrine Narducci (Rosina Anello).

1994
Mary Shelley's Frankenstein

Directed by Kenneth Branagh

Screenplay Frank Darabont, Steph Lady, from the novel by Mary Shelley *Cinematography* Roger Pratt *Set Decoration* Peter Francis *Original Music* Patrick Doyle *Film Editing* Andrew Marcus *Produced by* Francis Ford Coppola, James V. Hart, John Veitch. With Robert De Niro (The Creature), Kenneth Branagh (Victor Frankenstein), Tom Hulce (Henry Clerval), Helena Bonham Carter (Elizabeth), Aidan Quinn (Captain Robert Walton), Ian Holm (Baron Frankenstein), John Cleese (Professor Waldman).

1995
Les cent et une nuits de Simon Cinéma (One Hundred and One Nights)

Directed by Agnès Varda *Screenplay* Agnès Varda *Cinematography* Eric Gautier *Film Editing* Hugues Darmois *Produced by* Dominique Vignet. Robert De Niro plays a cameo role. Other performing participants in the fictional commemoration of the 100th anniversary of cinema are Michel Piccoli, Marcello Mastroianni, Anouk Aimée, Jean-Paul Belmondo, Alain Delon, Catherine Deneuve, Gérard Depardieu, Harrison Ford, Clint Eastwood, Gina Lollobrigida, and many more.

Casino

Directed by Martin Scorsese *Screenplay* Nicholas Pileggi, Martin Scorsese, from a book by Pileggi *Cinematography* Robert Richardson *Set Decoration* Omar Abderrahman *Film Editing* Thelma Schoonmaker *Produced by* Barbara De Fina. With Robert De Niro (Sam "Ace" Rothstein), Sharon Stone (Ginger McKenna), Joe Pesci (Nicky Santoro), James Woods (Lester Diamond), Frank Vincent (Frank Marino), Kevin Pollak (Phillip Green), Don Rickles (Billy Sherbert), L. Q. Jones (Pat Webb), Dick Smothers (Senator).

Heat

Directed by Michael Mann *Screenplay* Michael Mann *Cinematography* Dante Spinotti *Set Decoration* Anne H. Ahrens *Original Music* Elliot Goldenthal *Film Editing* Pasquale Buba, William Goldenberg, Dov Hoenig, Tom Rolf *Produced by* Art Linson, Michael Mann. With Al Pacino (Lt. Vincent Hanna), Robert De Niro (Neil McCauley), Val Kilmer (Chris Shiherlis), Jon Voight (Nate), Tom Sizemore (Michael Cheritto), Diane Venora (Justine Hanna), Ashley Judd (Charlene Shiherlis), Mykelti Williamson (Sergeant Drucker), Wes Studi (Detective Casals), Ted Levine (Bosko), Dennis Haysbert (Donald Breedan), Tom Noonan (Kelso), William Fichtner (Roger Van Zant), Natalie Portman (Lauren Gustafson), Hank Azaria (Alan Marciano).

1996
The Fan

Directed by Tony Scott *Screenplay* Phoef Sutton, from a novel by Peter Abrahams *Cinematography* Dariusz Wolski *Set Decoration* Claire Bowin *Original Music* Hans Zimmer *Film Editing* Claire Simpson, Christian Wagner *Produced by* Wendy Finerman, Margaret French-Isaac. With Robert De Niro (Gil Renard), Wesley Snipes (Bobby Rayburn), Ellen Barkin (Jewel Stern), John Leguizamo (Manny), Benicio Del Toro (Juan Primo), Patti D'Arbanville (Ellen Renard), Chris Mulkey (Tim).

Sleepers

Directed by Barry Levinson *Screenplay* Barry Levinson, from a book by Lorenzo Carcaterra *Cinematography* Michael Ballhaus *Set Decoration* Beth A. Rubino *Original Music* John Williams *Film Editing* Stu Linder *Produced by* Barry Levinson, Steve Golin, Lorenzo Carcaterra. With Kevin Bacon

(Sean Nokes), Billy Crudup (Tommy Marcano), Jason Patric (Lorenzo "Shakes" Carcaterra), Ron Eldard (John Reilly), Vittorio Gassman (King Benny), Minnie Driver (Carol Martinez), Robert De Niro (Father Bobby), Bruno Kirby (Shakes's Father), Dustin Hoffman (Danny Snyder).

Marvin's Room
Directed by Jerry Zaks *Screenplay* Scott McPherson, from his play *Cinematography* Piotr Sobocinski *Set Decoration* Tracey A. Doyle *Original Music* Rachel Portman *Film Editing* Jim Clark *Produced by* Scott Rudin, Jane Rosenthal, Robert De Niro. With Meryl Streep (Lee), Leonardo DiCaprio (Hank), Diane Keaton (Bessie), Robert De Niro (Dr. Wally), Hume Cronyn (Marvin), Gwen Verdon (Ruth), Dan Hedaya (Bob), Margo Martindale (Dr. Charlotte).

1997
Cop Land
Directed by James Mangold *Screenplay* James Mangold *Cinematography* Eric Alan Edwards *Set Decoration* Karen Wiesel *Original Music* Howard Shore *Film Editing* Craig McKay *Produced by* Cathy Konrad, Ezra Swerdlow, Cary Woods, Kerry Orent. With Sylvester Stallone (Freddy Heflin), Harvey Keitel (Ray Donlan), Ray Liotta (Gary Figgis), Robert De Niro (Moe Tilden), Peter Berg (Joey Randone), Janeane Garofalo (Deputy Cindy Betts), Robert Patrick (Jack Rucker), Michael Rapaport (Murray Babitch), Annabella Sciorra (Liz Randone), Cathy Moriarty (Rose Donlan), John Spencer (Leo Crasky), Frank Vincent (PDA President Lassaro).

Wag the Dog
Directed by Barry Levinson *Screenplay* Hilary Henkin, David Mamet, from a novel by Larry Beinhart *Cinematography* Robert

Richardson *Set Decoration* Robert Greenfield *Original Music* Mark Knopfler *Film Editing* Stu Linder *Produced by* Barry Levinson, Jane Rosenthal, Robert De Niro. With Robert De Niro (Conrad Brean), Dustin Hoffman (Stanley Motss), Anne Heche (Winifred Ames), William H. Macy (CIA Agent Charles Young), Denis Leary (Fad King), Willie Nelson (Johnny Dean), Kirsten Dunst (Tracy Lime), Andrea Martin (Liz Butsky), Woody Harrelson (Sergeant William Schumann).

Jackie Brown
Directed by Quentin Tarantino *Screenplay* Quentin Tarantino, from a novel by Elmore Leonard *Cinematography* Guillermo Navarro *Set Decoration* Sandy Reynolds-Wasco *Film Editing* Sally Menke *Produced by* Lawrence Bender, Paul Hellerman. With Pam Grier (Jackie Brown), Samuel L. Jackson (Ordell Robbie), Robert Forster (Max Cherry), Bridget Fonda (Melanie Ralston), Michael Keaton (Ray Nicolette), Robert De Niro (Louis Gara).

1998
Great Expectations
Directed by Alfonso Cuarón *Screenplay* Mitch Glazer, from the novel by Charles Dickens *Cinematography* Emmanuel Lubezki *Set Decoration* Susan Bode *Original Music* Patrick Doyle, Ron Wasserman *Film Editing* Steven Weisberg *Produced by* Art Linson, John Linson. With Ethan Hawke (Finnegan Bell), Gwyneth Paltrow (Estella), Hank Azaria (Walter Plane), Chris Cooper (Joe), Robert De Niro (Prisoner/Lustig), Anne Bancroft (Ms. Dinsmoor).

Ronin
Directed by John Frankenheimer *Screenplay* J. D. Zeik, Richard Weisz (David Mamet) *Cinematography* Robert Fraisse *Set Decoration* Robert Le Corre *Original*

Music Elia Cmiral *Film Editing* Tony Gibbs *Produced by* Frank Mancuso Jr. With Robert De Niro (Sam), Jean Reno (Vincent), Natascha McElhone (Deirdre), Stellan Skarsgård (Gregor), Sean Bean (Spence), Michael Lonsdale (Jean-Pierre), Jonathan Pryce (Seamus).

1999
Analyze This
Directed by Harold Ramis *Screenplay* Peter Tolan, Kenneth Lonergan, Harold Ramis *Cinematography* Stuart Dryburgh *Set Decoration* Leslie E. Rollins *Original Music* Howard Shore *Film Editing* Craig P. Herring, Christopher Tellefsen *Produced by* Jane Rosenthal, Paula Weinstein, Len Amato. With Robert De Niro (Paul Vitti), Billy Crystal (Dr. Ben Sobel), Lisa Kudrow (Laura MacNamara Sobel), Chazz Palminteri (Primo Sidone), Molly Shannon (Caroline), Bill Macy (Dr. Isaac Sobel), Pat Cooper (Salvatore Masiello).

Flawless
Directed by Joel Schumacher *Screenplay* Joel Schumacher *Cinematography* Declan Quinn *Set Decoration* Leslie Pope *Original Music* Bruce Roberts *Film Editing* Mark Stevens *Produced by* Jane Rosenthal, Caroline Baron, Joel Schumacher, Robert De Niro (uncredited). With Robert De Niro (Walt Koontz), Philip Seymour Hoffman (Rusty), Barry Miller (Leonard Wilcox), Daphne Rubin-Vega (Tia).

2000
The Adventures of Rocky and Bullwinkle
Directed by Des McAnuff *Screenplay* Kenneth Lonergan, based on characters created by Jay Ward *Cinematography* Thomas Ackerman *Set Decoration* Hilton Rosemarin *Original Music* Mark Mothersbaugh *Film Editing* Dennis Virkler *Produced by* Allison P. Brown (segment

producer), Jane Rosenthal, Robert De Niro, Brad Epstein. With Rene Russo (Natasha), Jason Alexander (Boris), June Foray (voice of Rocky, others), Keith Scott (voice of Bullwinkle, others), Piper Perabo (Karen Sympathy), Rod Biermann (Ole), Robert De Niro (Fearless Leader).

Men of Honor
Directed by George Tillman Jr. *Screenplay* Scott Marshall Smith *Cinematography* Anthony B. Richmond *Set Decoration* Kate J. Sullivan *Original Music* Mark Isham *Film Editing* John Carter, Dirk Westervelt *Produced by* Bill Badalato, Bill Cosby, Robert Teitel. With Cuba Gooding Jr. (Chief Carl Brashear), Robert De Niro (Master Chief Billy Sunday), Charlize Theron (Gwen Sunday), Aunjanue Ellis (Jo), Hal Holbrook ("Mr. Pappy"), Michael Rapaport (GM1 Snowhill), Powers Boothe (Captain Pullman).

Meet the Parents
Directed by Jay Roach *Screenplay* Jim Herzfeld and John Hamburg, based on characters and a story by Greg Glienna and Mary Ruth Clarke *Cinematography* Peter James *Set Decoration* Karin Wiesel *Original Music* Randy Newman *Film Editing* Greg Hayden, Jon Poll *Produced by* Nancy Tenenbaum, Jane Rosenthal, Jay Roach, Robert De Niro. With Ben Stiller (Gaylord "Greg" Focker), Robert De Niro (Jack Byrnes), Teri Polo (Pam Byrnes), Blythe Danner (Dina Byrnes), Owen Wilson (Kevin Rawley), James Rebhorn (Dr. Larry Banks).

2001
15 Minutes
Directed by John Herzfeld *Screenplay* John Herzfeld *Cinematography* Jean-Yves Escoffier *Set Decoration* Casey Hallenbeck *Original Music* Anthony Marinelli, J. Peter Robinson *Film Editing* Steven Cohen *Produced by* Keith

Addis, David Blocker, Nick Wechsler, John Herzfeld. With Robert De Niro (Detective Eddie Flemming), Edward Burns (Jody Warsaw), Kelsey Grammer (Robert Hawkins), Avery Brooks (Detective Leon Jackson), Vera Farmiga (Daphne Handlova).

The Score
Directed by Frank Oz *Screenplay* Kario Salem, Lem Dobbs, Scott Marshall Smith *Cinematography* Rob Hahn *Set Decoration* K. C. Fox *Original Music* Howard Shore *Film Editing* Richard Pearson *Produced by* Gary Foster, Lee Rich. With Robert De Niro (Nick Wells), Edward Norton, (Jack Teller), Marlon Brando (Max), Angela Bassett (Diane).

2002
Showtime
Directed by Tom Dey *Screenplay* Keith Sharon, Alfred Gough, Miles Millar *Cinematography* Thomas Kloss *Set Decoration* Tessa Posnansky *Original Music* Alan Silvestri *Film Editing* Billy Weber *Produced by* Jane Rosenthal, Jorge Saralegui. With Robert De Niro (Det. Mitch Preston), Eddie Murphy (Officer Trey Sellars), Mos Def (Lazy Boy), Rene Russo (Chase Renzi).

City by the Sea
Directed by Michael Caton-Jones *Screenplay* Ken Hixon *Cinematography* Karl Walter Lindenlaub *Set Decoration* Lynn Tonnessen *Original Music* John Murphy *Film Editing* Jim Clark *Produced by* Matthew Baer, Brad Grey, Elie Samaha, Michael Caton-Jones. With Robert De Niro (Vincent LaMarca) Frances McDormand (Michelle), James Franco (Joey), Eliza Dushku (Gina), Patti LuPone (Maggie).

Analyze That
Directed by Harold Ramis. *Screenplay* Peter Steinfeld, Harold Ramis, Peter Tolan

Cinematography Ellen Kuras *Set Decoration* Beth Rubino *Original Music* David Holmes *Film Editing* Andrew Mondshein *Produced by* Jane Rosenthal, Paula Weinstein, Suzanne Herrington. With Robert De Niro (Paul Vitti), Billy Crystal (Ben Sobel), Lisa Kudrow (Laura Sobel), Cathy Moriarty (Patti LoPresti).

2004
Godsend
Directed by Nick Hamm *Screenplay* Mark Bomback *Cinematography* Kramer Morgenthau *Set Decoration* Amanda Carroll, Nigel Hutchins, Susan Ogu *Original Music* Brian Tyler *Film Editing* Niven Howie, Steve Mirkovich *Produced by* Cathy Schulman, Mark Butan, Sean O'Keefe. With Greg Kinnear (Paul Duncan), Rebecca Romijn (Jessie Duncan), Robert De Niro (Richard Wells).

Shark Tale (Animated)
Directed by Bibo Bergeron, Vicky Jenson, Rob Letterman *Screenplay* Michael J. Wilson, Rob Letterman *Original Music* Hans Zimmer *Film Editing* Nick Fletcher, Peter Lonsdale, John Venzon *Produced by* Bill Damaschke, Janet Healy, Allison Lyon Segan. With the voice talent of Will Smith (Oscar), Robert De Niro (Don Lino), Renée Zellweger (Angie), Jack Black (Lenny), Angelina Jolie (Lola).

Meet the Fockers
Directed by Jay Roach *Screenplay* Jim Herzfeld, John Hamburg *Cinematography* John Schwartzman *Set Decoration* Sara Andrews *Original Music* Randy Newman *Film Editing* Alan Baumgarten, Lee Haxall, Jon Poll *Produced by* Robert DeNiro, Jay Roach, Jane Rosenthal. With Ben Stiller (Greg Focker), Robert De Niro (Jack Byrnes), Dustin Hoffman (Bernie Focker), Barbra Streisand (Rozalin Focker), Blythe Danner (Dina Byrnes),

Teri Polo (Pam Byrnes), Owen Wilson (Kevin Rawley).

The Bridge of San Luis Rey
Directed by Mary McGuckian *Screenplay* Mary McGuckian, from the novel by Thornton Wilder *Cinematography* Javier Aguirresarobe *Original Music* Lalo Schifrin *Film Editing* Kant Pan *Produced by* Michael Cowan, Samuel Hadida, Garrett McGuckian, Mary McGuckian, Denise O'Dell. With F. Murray Abraham (Viceroy of Peru), Kathy Bates (The Marquesa), Gabriel Byrne (Brother Juniper), Geraldine Chaplin (The Abbess), Robert De Niro (Archbishop of Peru), Harvey Keitel (Uncle Pio).

2005
Hide and Seek
Directed by John Polson *Screenplay* Ari Schlossberg *Cinematography* Dariusz Wolski *Set Decoration* Beth Kushnick *Original Music* John Ottman *Film Editing* Jeffrey Ford *Produced by* Barry Josephson, Dana Robin, John P. Rogers. With Robert De Niro (David Callaway), Dakota Fanning (Emily Callaway), Famke Janssen (Katherine), Elisabeth Shue (Elizabeth), Amy Irving (Alison Callaway), Dylan Baker (Sheriff Hafferty), Melissa Leo (Laura).

2006
Arthur and the Invisibles (Animated; English language version only)
Directed by Luc Besson *Screenplay* Céline Garcia, Luc Besson, from a book by Besson, based on characters created by Patrice Garcia, Georges Bouchelagem, Philippe Rouchier, Nicholas Fructus *Cinematography* Thierry Arbogast *Original Music* Eric Serra *Film Editing* Karim Benhammouda, Yann Hervé, Vincent Tabaillon *Produced by* Luc Besson, Emmanuel Prévost, Jérome de Baecque (animation producer). With the voice talent of

Freddie Highmore (Arthur), Mia Farrow (Granny), Robert De Niro (King), David Bowie (Maltazard), David Suchet (Narrator), others.

The Good Shepherd
Directed by Robert De Niro *Screenplay* Eric Roth *Cinematography* Robert Richardson *Set Decoration* Gretchen Rau, Leslie E. Rollins, Alyssa Winter *Original Music* Bruce Fowler, Marcelo Zarvos *Film Editing* Tariq Anwar *Produced by* Robert De Niro, Jane Rosenthal, James G. Robinson. With Matt Damon (Edward Wilson), Angelina Jolie (Margaret "Clover" Russell), Alec Baldwin (Sam Murach), Billy Crudup (Arch Cummings), Robert De Niro (Bill Sullivan), Keir Dullea (Senator John Russell Sr.), William Hurt (Philip Allen), Timothy Hutton (Thomas Wilson), Joe Pesci (Joseph Palmi).

2007
Stardust
Directed by Matthew Vaughn *Screenplay* Matthew Vaughn, Jane Goldman, from the novel by Neil Gaiman *Cinematography* Ben Davis *Set Decoration* Peter Young. *Original Music* Ilan Eshkeri *Film Editing* Jon Harris *Produced by* Lorenzo di Bonaventura, Michael Dreyer, Neil Gaiman, Matthew Vaughn, Chantal Feghali. With Claire Danes (Yvaine), Charlie Cox (Tristan Thorn), Michelle Pfeiffer (Lamia), Henry Cavill (Humphrey), Sienna Miller (Victoria), Robert De Niro (Captain Shakespeare).

2008
What Just Happened
Directed by Barry Levinson *Screenplay* Art Linson, from his book *Cinematography* Stéphane Fontaine *Set Decoration* Roya Parivar *Original Music* Marcelo Zarvos *Film Editing* Hank Corwin *Produced by* Barry Levinson, Art Linson, Robert

De Niro, Jane Rosenthal. With Robert De Niro (Ben), Sean Penn (Sean Penn), Catherine Keener (Lou Tarnow), John Turturro (Dick Bell), Robin Wright (Kelly), Stanley Tucci (Scott Solomon), Bruce Willis (Actor).

Righteous Kill
Directed by Jon Avnet *Screenplay* Russell Gewirtz *Cinematography* Denis Lenoir *Set Decoration* Kathy Lucas *Original Music* Edward Shearmur *Film Editing* Paul Hirsch *Produced by* Jon Avnet, Rob Cowan, Randall Emmett, Lati Grobman, Avi Lerner, Alexandra Milchan, Daniel M. Rosenberg. With Al Pacino (Rooster), Robert De Niro (Turk), Curtis Jackson (Spider), Carla Gugino (Karen Corelli), John Leguizamo (Det. Simon Perez), Donnie Wahlberg (Det. Ted Riley), Brian Dennehy (Hingis).

2009
Everybody's Fine
Directed by Kirk Jones *Screenplay* Kirk Jones, from an original screenplay by Giuseppe Tornatore, Tonino Guerra, Massimo De Rita *Cinematography* Henry Braham *Set Decoration* Chryss Hionis *Original Music* Dario Marianelli *Film Editing* Andrew Mondshein *Produced by* Vittorio Cecchi Gori, Ted Field, Glynis Murray, Gianni Nunnari. With Robert De Niro (Frank Goode), Drew Barrymore (Rosie), Kate Beckinsale (Amy), Sam Rockwell (Robert).

2010
Machete
Directed by Robert Rodriguez, Ethan Maniquis *Screenplay* Robert Rodriguez, Álvaro Rodríguez *Cinematography* Jimmy Lindsey *Set Decoration* Bart Brown. *Original Music* Chingon *Film Editing* Robert Rodriguez, Rebecca Rodriguez *Produced by* Elizabeth Avellan, Rick Schwartz, Robert Rodriguez. With Danny Trejo (Machete), Jessica Alba (Sartana), Robert De Niro (Senator John McLaughlin), Cheech Marin (Padre).

Stone
Directed by John Curran *Screenplay* Angus MacLachlan, from his play *Cinematography* Maryse Alberti *Set Decoration* James V. Kent *Film Editing* Alexandre de Franceschi *Produced by* David Mimran, Jordan Schur, Holly Wiersma. With Robert De Niro (Jack Mabry), Edward Norton (Gerald "Stone" Creeson), Milla Jovovich (Lucetta Creeson), Frances Conroy (Madylyn Mabry).

Little Fockers
Directed by Paul Weitz *Screenplay* John Hamburg, Larry Stuckey *Cinematography* Remi Adefarasin *Set Decoration* David Smith *Original Music* Stephen Trask *Film Editing* Greg Hayden, Leslie Jones, Myron I. Kerstein *Produced by* Robert De Niro, John Hamburg, Jay Roach, Jane Rosenthal. With Ben Stiller (Greg Focker), Robert De Niro (Jack Byrnes), Dustin Hoffman (Bernie Focker), Barbra Streisand (Roz Focker), Blythe Danner (Dina Byrnes), Teri Polo (Pam Focker), Jessica Alba (Andi Garcia).

2011
Manual d'amore (*The Age of Love*)
Directed by Giovanni Veronesi *Screenplay* Giovanni Veronesi, Ugo Chiti *Cinematography* Giovanni Canevari *Film Editing* Patrizio Marone *Produced by* Luigi De Laurentiis Jr., Aurelio De Laurentiis. With Monica Bellucci (Viola), Riccardo Scamarcio (Roberto), Robert De Niro (Adrian).

Limitless
Directed by Neil Burger *Screenplay* Leslie Dixon, from a novel by Alan Glynn *Cinematography* Jo Willems *Set Decoration* Diane Lederman *Original Music* Paul Leonard-Morgan *Film Editing* Tracy Adams, Naomi Geraghty *Produced by* Ryan Kavanaugh, Scott Kroopf, Leslie Dixon. With Bradley Cooper (Eddie Morra), Abbie Cornish (Lindy), Anna Friel (Melissa), Robert De Niro (Carl Van Loon).

Killer Elite
Directed by Gary McKendry *Screenplay* Matt Sherring, from a book by Ranulph Fiennes *Cinematography* Simon Duggan *Set Decoration* Rolland Pike, Aziz Hamichi *Original Music* Reinhold Heil, Johnny Klimek *Film Editing* John Gilbert *Produced by* Bénédicte Bellocq, Michael Boughen, Steve Chasman, Sigurjon Sighvatsson, Tony Winley. With Jason Statham (Danny), Clive Owen (Spike), Robert De Niro (Hunter).

New Year's Eve
Directed by Garry Marshall *Screenplay* Katherine Fugate *Cinematography* Charles Minsky *Set Decoration* Leslie E. Rollins *Original Music* John Debney *Film Editing* Michael Tronick *Produced by* Garry Marshall, Toby Emmerich, Mike Karz, Wayne Allan Rice, Josie Rosen, Heather Hall. With Halle Berry (Nurse Aimee), Cary Elwes (Stan's Doctor), Alyssa Milano (Nurse Mindy), Common (Soldier), Robert De Niro (Stan Harris), Hilary Swank (Claire Morgan).

2012
Red Lights
Directed by Rodrigo Cortés *Screenplay* Rodrigo Cortés *Cinematography* Xavi Giménez *Original Music* Victor Reyes *Film Editing* Rodrigo Cortés *Produced by* Rodrigo Cortés, Adrián Guerra, Christina Piovesan, Manuel Monzón. With Cillian Murphy (Tom Buckley), Sigourney Weaver (Margaret Matheson) Robert De Niro (Simon Silver), Toby Jones (Paul Shackleton), Joely Richardson (Monica Hansen).

Being Flynn
Directed by Paul Weitz *Screenplay* Paul Weitz, from a book by Nick Flynn *Cinematography* Declan Quinn *Set Decoration* Susan Perlman *Original Music* Badly Drawn Boy *Film Editing* Joan Sobel *Produced by* Michael Costigan, Andrew Miano, Paul Weitz, Dan Balgoyen. With Paul Dano (Nick Flynn) Robert De Niro (Jonathan Flynn), Olivia Thirlby (Denise), Lili Taylor (Joy), Julianne Moore (Jody Flynn).

Freelancers
Directed by Jessy Terrero *Screenplay* L. Philippe Casseus *Cinematography* Igor Martinovic *Set Decoration* Monique Champagne *Original Music* Reg B. *Film Editing* Sean Albertson, Sara Mineo, Kirk M. Morri *Produced by* Curtis "50 Cent" Jackson, Randall Emmett, George Furia. With Curtis "50 Cent" Jackson (Malo), Forest Whitaker (LaRue), Robert De Niro (Joe Sarcone).

Silver Linings Playbook
Directed by David O. Russell *Screenplay* David O. Russell, from a novel by Matthew Quick *Cinematography* Masanobu Takayanagi *Set Decoration* Heather Loeffler *Original Music* Danny Elfman *Film Editing* Jay Cassidy, Crispin Struthers *Produced by* Bruce Cohen, Donna Gigliotti, Jonathan Gordon, Mark Kamine. With Bradley Cooper (Pat), Jennifer Lawrence (Tiffany), Robert De Niro (Pat Sr.), Jacki Weaver (Dolores), Chris Tucker (Danny).

2013
The Big Wedding
Directed by Justin Zackham *Screenplay* Justin Zackham, from a screenplay by Jean-Stéphane Bron and Karine Sudan *Cinematography*

Jonathan Brown *Set Decoration* David Schlesinger *Original Music* Nathan Barr *Film Editing* Jon Corn *Produced by* Anthony Katagas, Clay Pecorin, Richard Salvatore, Harry J. Ufland, Justin Zackham. With Amanda Seyfried (Missy), Diane Keaton (Ellie), Susan Sarandon (Bebe) Robert De Niro (Don), Topher Grace (Jared), Katherine Heigl (Lyla), Robin Williams (Father Moinighan).

Killing Season
Directed by Mark Steven Johnson *Screenplay* Evan Daugherty *Cinematography* Peter Menzies Jr. *Set Decoration* Melinda Sanders *Original Music* Christopher Young *Film Editing* Sean Albertson *Produced by* Paul Breuls, Ed Cathell III, Anthony Rhulen, John Thompson. With Robert De Niro (Benjamin Ford), John Travolta (Emil Kovac), Milo Ventimiglia (Chris Ford).

The Family
Directed by Luc Besson *Screenplay* Luc Besson, Michael Caleo, from a book by Tonino Benacquista *Cinematography* Thierry Arbogast *Set Decoration* Cherish Magennis, Evelyne Tissandier *Original Music* Evgueni Galperine, Sacha Galperine *Film Editing* Julien Rey *Produced by* Luc Besson, Ryan Kavanaugh, Virginie Silla. With Robert De Niro (Fred Blake/Giovanni Manzoni), Michelle Pfeiffer (Maggie Blake), Tommy Lee Jones (Robert Stansfield).

Last Vegas
Directed by Jon Turteltaub *Screenplay* Dan Fogelman *Cinematography* David Hennings *Set Decoration* Patrick Cassidy *Original Music* Mark Mothersbaugh. *Film Editing* David Rennie *Produced by* Amy Baer, Joseph Drake, Laurence Mark. With Robert De Niro (Paddy), Morgan Freeman (Archie), Michael Douglas (Billy), Kevin Kline (Sam), Mary Steenburgen (Diana).

Grudge Match
Directed by Peter Segal *Screenplay* Tim Kelleher, Rodney Rothman. *Cinematography* Dean Semler *Set Decoration* Matt Callahan *Original Music* Trevor Rabin *Film Editing* William Kerr *Produced by* Michael Ewing, Bill Gerber, Mark Steven Johnson, Ravi D. Mehta, Peter Segal. With Robert De Niro (Billy "The Kid" McDonnen), Sylvester Stallone (Henry "Razor" Sharp), Kim Basinger (Sally Rose), Kevin Hart (Dante Slate Jr.), Alan Arkin (Lightning).

American Hustle
Directed by David O. Russell *Screenplay* Eric Singer, David O. Russell *Cinematography* Linus Sandgren *Set Decoration* Heather Loeffler *Film Editing* Jay Cassidy *Produced by* Megan Ellison, Charles Rovin, Richard Suckle. With Robert De Niro (Victor Tellegio), Christian Bale (Irving Rosenfeld), Jennifer Lawrence (Rosalyn Rosenfeld), Bradley Cooper (Richie DiMaso), Amy Adams (Sydney Prosser).

2014
The Bag Man
Directed by David Grovic *Screenplay* Paul Conway, David Grovic, James Russo *Cinematography* Steve Mason *Set Decoration* Cynthia Anne Slagter *Original Music* Tony Morales, Edward Rogers *Film Editing* Devin Maurer, Michael R. Miller *Produced by* Peter D. Graves, Warren Ostergard. With Robert De Niro, John Cusack, Crispin Glover.

De Niro as Al Capone in *The Untouchables* (1987), directed by Brian De Palma.

Bibliography

Articles

Patricia Bosworth, "The
  Shadow King," *Vanity Fair*,
  October 1987.
Stephen Garrett, "It's Payback
  Time," *Time Out New
  York*, May 9–16, 2002.
Lawrence Grobel, "Robert
  De Niro: The Playboy
  Interview," *Playboy*,
  January 1989.
Tom Topor, "He Had To Play
  Ball," *The New York Post*,
  August 25, 1973.
Nick Tosches, "Bobby's
  Back," *Esquire*, UK edition,
  March 1996.

Books

John Baxter, *De Niro: A
  Biography*, HarperCollins,
  London, 2002.
John Boorman and Walter
  Donahue, eds., *Projections
  7*, Faber and Faber,
  London, 1997.
Ian Christie and David
  Thompson, *Scorsese on
  Scorsese*, Faber and Faber,
  London, 2003.
Andy Dougan, *Untouchable:
  A Biography of Robert De
  Niro*, Thunder's Mouth
  Press, New York, 1997.
Manny Farber, *Farber on
  Film*, Library of America,
  New York, 2009.
Elia Kazan, *A Life*, Alfred A.
  Knopf, New York, 1988.
Michael Henry Wilson,
  Scorsese on Scorsese,
  Cahiers du Cinema,
  London/New York, 2011.

1 Michael Powell, *Million Dollar Movie*, Random House, 1995, p. 560

2 *Scorsese on Scorsese*, eds. Ian Christie and David Thompson, Faber and Faber, 2003, p. 84.

3 Powell, *op. cit.*, p. 560.

4 "Robert De Niro… private, professional, a male Greta Garbo," tagline "N.C.," W, July 11, 1975

5 Nick Tosches, *The Nick Tosches Reader*, Da Capo, 2000, p. 435.

6 Elia Kazan, *A Life*, Alfred A. Knopf, 1988, p. 766.

7 *Ibid.*, p. 766.

8 Gilbert Adair, *Flickers: An Illustrated Celebration of 100 Years of Cinema*, Faber and Faber, 1995, p. 172.

9 Christie and Thompson, *op. cit.*, p. 42

10 Lawrence Grobel, "The Playboy Interview: Robert De Niro," *Playboy*, January 1989.

11 Patrick McGilligan, "Night Shooting in NYC with Martin Scorsese," *Boston Sunday Globe*, August 17, 1975.

12 Liz Smith, column, New York *Newsday*, October 31, 2003.

13 Gene S. Key, "*Tchin-Tchin*," *Guilford Gazette*, May 3, 1967.

14 John Baxter, *Robert De Niro: A Biography*, HarperCollins (London), 2002, p. 54.

15 *Ibid.*, p. 53.

16 *Ibid.*, p. 56.

17 *Ibid.*, p. 98.

18 Jim Bouton, "Bang the Drum, Loudly," *The New York Times*, September 30, 1973.

19 "Dialogue on Film," unsigned, *American Film*, March 1981.

20 Tom Topor, "He Had to Play Ball," *The New York Post*, August 25, 1973.

21 Baxter, *op. cit.*, pp. 366–367.

22 Margaret Roman, "The Eye," *Scholastic Scope*, October 4, 1973.

23 Herbert Mitgang, "From Yale to the Ball Park, Good Conduct Is What Counts," *The New York Times*, December 2, 1988.

24 Grobel, *op. cit.*

25 Christie and Thompson, *op. cit.*, p. 38.

26 From "De Niro and Me," Martin Scorsese, in *Projections 7*, eds. John Boorman and Walter Donahue, Faber and Faber, 1997, p. 38.

27 Christie and Thompson, *op. cit.*, p. 43.

28 Michael Henry Wilson, *Scorsese on Scorsese*, Cahiers du Cinema, 2011, p. 35.

29 Christie and Thompson, *op. cit.*, p. 43.

30 Andy Dougan, *Untouchable: A Biography of Robert De Niro*, Thunder's Mouth Press, New York, 1997, p. 57.

31 Robert Evans, *The Kid Stays in the Picture*, Hyperion, p. 218.

32 Baxter, *op. cit.*, p. 116.

33 Grobel, *op. cit.*

34 Peter Cowie, *The Godfather Book*, Faber and Faber, 1997, p. 84.

35 Peter Biskind, *The Godfather Companion*, 1990, Harper Perennial, p. 85.

36 Mason Wiley and Damien Bona, *Inside Oscar, 10th Anniversary Edition*, Ballantine Books, 1996, p. 501.

37 *Ibid.*, p. 504.

38 Grobel, *op. cit.*

39 Richard Thompson, "Writer Paul Schrader," *Film Comment*, April–May 1976.

40 Christie and Thompson, *op. cit.*, p. 54.

41 Dougan, *op. cit.*, p. 80.

42 *Ibid.*, p. 75.

43 Ian Christie and David Thompson, *op. cit.*, p. 54.

44 Boorman and Donahue, *op. cit.*, p. 52.

45 Reprinted in *Farber on Film*, ed. Robert Polito, Library of America, 2009, p. 756.

46 "Dialogue on Film," *op. cit.*

47 Review of *Taxi Driver*, Vincent Canby, *The New York Times*, February 9, 1976.

48 Grobel, *op. cit.*

49 Clarence Clemons and Don Reo, *Big Man: Real Life & Tall Tales*, Grand Central Publishing, 2009, Kindle edition, locations 1553–1567.

50 Boorman and Donahue, *op. cit.*, p. 46.

51 Biskind, *op. cit.*, p. 387.

52 Mary Pat Kelly, *Scorsese: A Journey*, Thunder's Mouth Press, 1991, p. 126.

53 *Ibid.*, p. 135.

54 Christie and Thompson, *op. cit.*, p. 83.

55 "The Current Cinema: Religious Pulp, or The Incredible Hulk," Pauline Kael, *The New Yorker*, December 8, 1980, reprinted in Kael, *For Keeps: 30 Years at the Movies*, 1994, Dutton, p. 877.

56 Cited in David Ehrenstein, *The Scorsese Picture*, 1992, Birch Lane Press, p. 67.

57 Robin Wood, *Hollywood from Vietnam to Reagan*, 1986, Columbia University Press, p. 251.

58 *Ibid.*, p. 252.

59 Kelly, *op. cit.*, p. 126.

60 Powell, *op. cit.*, p. 567.

61 Wiley and Bona, *op. cit.*, p. 596.

62 *Ibid.*

63 Quoted in Baxter, *op. cit.*, p. 220.

64 Wilson, *op. cit.*, p. 111.

65 Schickel, *op. cit.*, p. 150.

66 Kelly, *op. cit.*, p. 154. The event De Niro recounts does not appear in the finished film.

67 Shawn Levy, *King of Comedy: The Life and Art of Jerry Lewis*, St. Martin's Griffin, 1996, p. 423.

68 Grobel, *op. cit.*

69 Pauline Kael, "The Current Cinema: Jokers," *The New Yorker*, March 7, 1983.

70 "Martin Scorsese and the Comedy of Public Life," *The Village Voice*,

Feb. 15, 1983, reprinted in J. Hoberman, *Vulgar Modernism: Writing on Movies and Other Media*, Temple University Press, 1991, p. 85.

71 "N.C.", *op. cit.* (see note 4).

72 Baxter, *op. cit.*, p. 238.

73 Charles Grodin, *It Would Be So Nice If You Weren't Here*, Vintage, 1989, p. 284.

74 *Ibid.*, p. 293.

75 Lawrence van Gelder, "A Question for De Niro," *The New York Times*, July 22, 1988.

76 Grodin, *op. cit.*, p. 289.

77 *Ibid.*

78 Andrew Sarris, "*Midnight Run*," *Video Review*, March 1989.

79 Harry Haun, "De Niro May Finally 'Run' Wild at the Box Office," *Daily News*, July 27, 1988.

80 Grobel, *op. cit.*

81 Boorman and Donahue, *op. cit.*, p. 55.

82 Oliver Sacks, *Awakenings*, E. P. Dutton, 1983, p. 195.

83 David Thomson, *A Biographical Dictionary of Film*, Third Edition, Knopf, 1994, p. 188.

84 Dougan, *op. cit.*, p. 214.

85 John C. Tibbetts, "Robert De Niro Talks About Role in 'This Boy's Life'," *The Christian Science Monitor*, April 23, 1993.

86 Baxter, *op. cit.*, p. 143

87 *Ibid.*, p. 271.

88 *Ibid.*, p. 368.

89 *Ibid.*, p. 370.

90 Stephen Garrett, "It's Payback Time," *Time Out New York*, May 9–16, 2002.

91 Terrence Rafferty, "A King of Comedy? Are You Talkin' About HIM?" *The New York Times*, Arts & Leisure section, November 3, 2002.

92 Edward Norton, interview with the author, April 5, 2013. All other Norton quotes from same.

93 Rachel Dodes, "Robert De Niro Can't Slow Down," *The Wall Street Journal*, April 6, 2012.

94 *Ibid.*

95 "N.C.," *op. cit.*

Sidebar Notes

a Gene S. Key, "*Tchin-Tchin*," Guilford Gazette, May 3, 1967

b John Baxter, *De Niro: A Biography*, HarperCollins, London, 2003, p. 255–256.

c Tom Topor, "He Had to Play Ball," *The New York Post*, August 25, 1973.

d Cal Fussman, "Robert De Niro: What I've Learned," *Esquire*, December 14, 2010.

e Martin Scorsese, "De Niro and Me," in *Projections 7*, eds. John Boorman and Walter Donohue, Faber and Faber, London, 1997.

f Baxter, *op.cit.*, p. 35.

g Edward Norton, interview with the author, April 5, 2013.

h *Ibid.*

De Niro as troubled Mafia boss Paul Vitti in Harold Ramis's *Analyze This* (1999).

Index

191

Original title: *Robert De Niro*
© 2014 Cahiers du cinéma
SARL

Titre original:
Robert De Niro © 2014
Cahiers du cinéma SARL

This Edition published by
Phaidon Press Limited
under licence from Cahiers
du cinéma SARL,
18-20, rue Claude-Tillier,
75012 Paris, France © 2014
Cahiers du cinéma SARL.

Cette Édition est publiée
par Phaidon Press Limited
avec l'autorisation des
Cahiers du cinéma SARL,
18-20, rue Claude-Tillier,
75012 Paris, France © 2014
Cahiers du cinéma SARL.

Cahiers du cinéma
18-20, rue Claude-Tillier
75012 Paris

www.cahiersducinema.com

ISBN 978 0 7148 6802 8

A CIP catalogue record of this
book is available from the
British Library.

Series concept designed
by Thomas Mayfried
Designed by Isobel Gillan

Printed in China

Acknowledgments

Thanks to the New York
Public Library for the
Performing Arts and its staff.
At Cahiers du cinéma: Valérie
Buffet, Amélie Despérier-
Bougdira, Anne McDowall,
Jérôme Cuzol, Laure Giroir.
Edward Norton and De Niro
biographer-in-progress Shawn
Levy were generous with their
time and insights.
For transcribing, thanks to
Jean Brown. I am grateful
to my friends Ron Goldberg
and Joseph Failla, with whom
I saw for the first time many
of the movies discussed here.
Zach Barocas, Jennifer Chi,
Kent Jones, Brian Koppelman,
and David Levien also helped
me. My wonderful wife Claire
Kenny was and is a constant
source of love, inspiration,
support, and insight.
I dedicate this book to my
parents, Allan Kenny and
Amelia Kenny.